Narrative Wilderness

Narrative Wilderness

BEING IN **TIME** AND **PLACE**

BONNIE DURRANCE

SHANTI ARTS PUBLISHING
BRUNSWICK, MAINE

Narrative Wilderness
Being in Time and Place

Copyright © 2025 Bonnie Durrance (text and photographs)

All Rights Reserved

Published by Shanti Arts Publishing

Cover and all interior images by Bonnie Durrance

Book design by John N. Bull, Publishing Art Australia

Shanti Arts LLC
193 Hillside Road
Brunswick, Maine 04011
shantiarts.com

While this book is a memoir, in that the events, people, and situations the author describes here have come forth from her memory, they have all been rendered in full for the page in the style of a work of creative nonfiction. Dialogue, for example, has been reconstructed from memory. Names have been changed. But the descriptions of the place, the situation, the story, the characters, both human and non-human, are all, in their essence, true. The coastal village where the action takes place is a real place, but un-named because when the author lived there, people wanted privacy. Now, thanks to the internet, the place is discovered. The author leaves it to readers so motivated to find out its name for themselves.

Printed in the United States of America

ISBN: 978-1-962082-50-1 (softcover)
ISBN: 978-1-962082-51-8 (ebook)

Library of Congress Control Number: 2024952536

For my beloved Robert

Contents

1
Hiding from Death in Joe's Taco Lounge 12
The Fault 14
Begin with Plants 17

2
How We Started 22

3
The Decision 30
A Building of One's Own 33

4
A Solitude of Two 38
The Practice of Paying Attention 39

5
Narrative Wilderness 46
The Refugee Gardener 48
Freedom in Context 51
Patterns of Recognition 53

6
The First Offer 58
The Nouveau Poor 62
The Origins of Squalor 64
The Monkey Trap 66
The Known and the Unknown 68
The Importance of Names 73
Mysteries of Time and Space 76

7

Seeing in the Dark 80

Living in Goodbye 83

This Moment in Time 85

The Joy of Dogs 87

8

The Shadow 92

Downtown 95

Mariah 98

Attitude Adjustment 100

Of Wild Men and Hardworking Animals 104

Liver Chi Backup 108

9

A Word about Sparrows 114

A Word about Loss 115

Night of the Broken Crockery 117

New Moon, New Men 122

10

The Lack of Raccoons 128

Mrs. Rocky's Tale 131

Goodbye Eyes 137

11

The Wedding Photographer 142

12

Gifts from Duxbury Reef 154

Reprieve 156

Easter Sunday 157

Notes 161

About the Author 165

Acknowledgements

No creative act, no matter how big or small, is done or completed alone. My first thanks for helping this book to get into your hands is for my friend and long-ago English teacher at Ursuline Academy in Bethesda, Maryland, Ginny Walsh Furtwangler (1932–2024). Shanti Arts published her memoir, *Music in Time*, one of her many books under the pen name, Ann Copeland, and she encouraged me to contact Shanti's wonderful Christine Cote about my book. So here we are. My deep appreciation for their support and encouragement to publish goes to my long-time friends, Prisca Crettier Weems, and photographers Philip Metcalf (1942–2019) and Patricia Galagan, his wife, a fellow Ursuline girl. I owe thanks also to Melba Patillo Beals, a powerful goddess woman, who inspired me with her story and encouraged me with mine. I am grateful, too, for the intrepid women of Napa Valley Scribblers, Jennifer Baerwald, Ann Newton Holmes and Molly Detwiler, whose smart readership and sharp editorial eyes make better whatever they read. I could not mention thanks without adding my sister, Diane McBride, whose creative advice is always wise, and David H. Lyman, who opened the door to the world of photography and taught me to see what I fear as a challenge.

1

Hiding from Death in Joe's Taco Lounge

Under any kind of death sentence, one's view of the world clears up. Once, being wheeled fast through the corridors of New York's Roosevelt Hospital into a room of metal and lights where masked men with scalpels raised were about to save my life, I saw, clearly, as if lit by a ray of sunlight, the moss on the rocks in the front of my home on the coast of Maine.

British soldiers they are called. Staunch little fellows. Red caps, mint-green stems, standing at attention, rain or shine. As the ceiling tiles of the corridor blurred by and the screen of my mind went white, I began to picture the little soldier mosses, living, being, breathing mist and sea. I heard an inner voice say, *I want to live,* as the mind screen was fading white, and the mirror people pressed the mask down over my nose, *and see the moss again, see it better, photograph it better next time...*

Once, sitting in a new friend's apartment in Midtown, his beautiful young wife, pausing her story about how she wished she'd become a biologist, asked if we'd mind if she removed her wig. We smiled, as though people, pushing back their chairs after dinner, said that all the time. Smiling, too, she raised her delicate arm, sunk her hand into her blonde pouf of hair, and pulled it off as one would a hat, and flung it across the room. Then, stroking her bald head, she said, big-eyed, sheepish, "You know, before this tumor, I had nothing in my head at all! Now, there is everything to do and no more time."

And so it feels here, a distance away in time and on the opposite coast. Here, I have everything to see and love and no more time.

I should be clear. The voice on the end of the phone that pronounced the dreaded sentence was not the doctor—I'm sorry, I have some bad news about your tests—nor the police—I'm sorry, there's been a terrible accident—but the real estate man. "Good news! I have some buyers for the house!"

He said he wants to bring them around at three. "Nice people," "prospective buyers," "new owners"—words like these, like clouds of bats' wings, fluttered through my brain. I wanted to place a cannon at the door. Rifles at all the windows. Land mines in the driveway. Anything. But the real estate man was only doing his job. And this death is but the death of a dream.

Today, the first prospective "buyers" would arrive to scrutinize the place. My husband and I, as new to each other as to this sort of hardship, fled separately from the scene, driving off in opposite directions to lose ourselves and our shame in the gray November rain.

I drove "over the hill" and ended up sloshing about in the village of Mill Valley, alone, thinking of what to do and where to go and realizing I had left the house with nothing to write on and nothing to read. So I went to the Depot bookstore, a place where locals read their poetry and hopeful artists hang pictures. I looked at all the work on the walls and all the successful faces on the book covers and, in a burst of full-blown self-hatred, bought a book on careers. I brought the book—bag and all—and slogged down the street, led by the blinking lights in the window of Joe's Taco Lounge. It was only 5 o'clock and the place was half empty. I sat down at one of the wildly colored, chintz-covered tables and decided that—hell with careers—at times like this one has to write.

"Here in Joe's Taco Lounge the dust is jumping," I scrawled on the brown paper bag. "Colors buzz, greens, reds, yellows, oranges, and the Gypsy Kings' samba music makes pogo sticks of every diner's spine. The wine is mellow and red and comforting, and my life is falling apart..." I began, getting into the scene and out of my life. A cute straw-haired guy sitting up at the counter turned and looked down at my table and winked at me as I scrawled my despair onto the bag. He had the young, blue-jean and boots swaggering looks that said he hadn't a care in the world, and his smile had a certain fondness for the world about it.

"Gotta catch that inspiration any way ya can, huh?"

"Right," I said. "Can't let these golden nuggets go by free." I smiled back as he eyed me and my un-Mill Valley garb.

"Got your mud boots on, huh?"

"Yeah," I said, looking down at my old Maine lobsterman's boots that made me swagger even sitting down.

"Where I live, there's lots of mud."

"Where's that?" What a nice smile, I thought. He's just a kid. Young,

Iowa kind of face, a face that has never been troubled by losing a home.

"Over the mountain," I said. "It's just over the mountain, on the edge of the sea. I live there." The sounds of those words escaped into the air, and I had to turn away because I didn't want this nice kid to see a person his mother's age cry. To steady myself, I focused my eyes on the menu and then decided that if I am about to shake hands with the unknown, I will begin with chalupas.

God is good.

The heavenly little morsels with their accompanying Merlot are singing in my memory now. The night and the rain and the clomping boots and the book on careers and my poor, terrified husband and the real estate man and his innocent clients—all of it, all of it was happening—the delicious, the terrible, the dreadful, and the great, like one big cacophonous opera that doesn't end, only quiets, at the end of the day.

A day I will have remembered, while in it.

The Fault

This area where we live is on the southern end of a long peninsula that lies parallel to and adjoining the California mainland. It is bounded to the west by the Pacific Ocean and to the southwest by the milelong Duxbury Reef, the largest shale reef in North America, according to my guidebook. Toward the southeast, sheltered by the reef, lies a gentle bay that feeds into a shallow lagoon and a harbor once used by whaling boats.

Back in the eighteenth century, before cattle ranchers and agriculture and logging began changing the landscape, the lagoon was teeming with birds, fish, and wildlife—even grizzlies and elk. The Coast Miwok people had lived along these shores undisturbed, in harmony with the nature of the place, for two thousand years before the first farmers came with their cattle and plows. With agriculture and settlement and logging, the nature of the place began a long series of changes. The mighty redwood forests across from the lagoon—some trees, it was written, measured fifty feet around—were clear-cut, the wood shipped across the Bay to San Francisco to build the shipping docks, and later, after the earthquake in 1906, to rebuild all of San Francisco. Runoff from the bare hills and the farmland up on the highland washed silt into the lagoon, and in time, the whaling boats could no longer sail into the harbor to load and unload their wares. All that now remains of the great ships and the whales is a small fleet of fishing boats, a seasonal supply of halibut, and a couple of sandbars used by sea lions to bask in the summer sun.

Through the center of the lagoon runs the San Andreas Fault, placing this area—fittingly, considering the independent stripe of its inhabitants—upon a geologic plate all its own. Stand on the edge of the cliff in the mist and you can feel it. The earth is chunky, cracked, disrupted from below. Big rifts buckle whole strips of ground and even rip up plants, leaving the land along the cliff with a sunken, multi-leveled appearance, like a pudding collapsed from within. This is where I walk, maybe one hundred feet above the sea, knowing each chunk of earth that my insignificant weight falls upon could at any moment lurch as the Pacific Plate inches north and collapse in an avalanche of clay and bramble, carrying rocks and plants—and possibly even me—down, down the cliff to the sea.

I came to this place, a place as fragile and tenacious as my own inner balance, by choice. I was at a point in my life like that place Dante describes—a dark wood, where a person in the middle of life feels lost and afraid, unable to go back and afraid to go forward. I came here, seeking refuge from a complicated life with a singular purpose: to learn to see clearly and to learn, if it's even possible, how to love. Susceptible as I was to internal pressures, I saw the stress of this place, with its steep edge, its imminent indications of change, its brave new blades of grass pushing out of the drought-cracked crust, as kindred. I saw my moods as landslides—surprise events that would happen in the depths when some strong force yanked loose a band of inner ground.

At such times, I could almost feel a whole bank of surface life collapse—plants, trees, roots, rocks, faith, belief, or certainty in anything—and with it any hope at all would give way to the moaning black and roiling sea. At the same time, I found that in each new cutaway of ground, something new could open to view. I began to see the place as a kind of Brigadoon, a place that lives somewhere beyond the rim of fog, where magic happens, if you let it, that only gets revealed from time to miraculous time. All I ever wanted, visible and invisible, I found here.

People like me, who seek a place like this, tend to have stories. Many have come with hopes, dreams, and wounds—mental, physical, spiritual—that need to heal. I was told by a massage therapist soon after I settled here that the original inhabitants knew this place as a healing ground. Come and do your healing, the stories go, but when you have healed, you must either become a healer or move on, or your "stitches" will unloose, and you may come undone. Fair warning, I thought. She made that twirling index finger at the temple gesture, rolling her eyes.

After living in this castaway place for a while, in a one-room studio with a great view, it occurred to me, observing the comings and goings of the denizens of the town, that one could come undone in a variety of ways. One person of local note dressed herself in burlap and newspapers with elaborate headdresses decorated and held together with braided twine holding dangling apples. In the town's one café, called "The Café," I once observed this character, up at the counter, as she was paying her bill and I had come up to pay mine. She was very small, and her leathery skin suggested that she was well on in life. She held in her hands a ballpoint pen and a small, neat checkbook with a leather cover. Her hands were sun-browned, unlined, and precise. I saw her write her name in a tight, neat script. She tore a check out carefully and handed it to the owner, a wry, tired woman whose round Slavic face, framed by gray-blonde bobbed hair, must have been beautiful in her youth. She greeted the strange customer with a kind smile and wished her a good day. The woman in her garb, with apples swinging from her headdress, nodded, turned, and shuffled toward the door, newspapers crackling. The room, dark, with wooden rafters and natural pine walls, was semifilled with diners, locals mostly, who paid no attention to the unique presence passing by them on the way to the door. Back at the register, I moved into the unique person's space, noticing the vaguely spicy smell her aura left. I put my bill on the counter together with my credit card and gave the owner a lift of the eyebrows. "She's off her medication," the owner said, gazing toward the door and the departing figure, with a "what can you do?" shrug.

Someone told me later that the strangely attired person had been a lawyer, in Boston. Maybe true, maybe not.

But whatever she was doing, in this odd, out-of-the-way town, she seemed to have found some freedom she needed, to be herself. There were others around, too, who defied diagnosis, but it's the one with the deliberate manner and the ingenious headdress who sticks in my mind. Her careful hand. Her dignity underneath her disguise.

My own disguise was the more normal kind. I had a camera, a red sports car, wore jeans and silk shirts, and was letting the perm wear out on my short, frizzed hair. How, after all, a continent away from civilization, can you think of finding a hairdresser? And besides, who cared? I'd come to be in the land and to find in the land those two essential capabilities without which life, for me, had no meaning. As I've said: to see clearly and to learn how to love. Easy. But how?

Begin with Plants

The Russian philosopher Gurdieff is said to have advised: To learn to love, begin with plants. Spare animals and other humans the insult of our expectations. Love needs acceptance. This is hard. Best to start with plants.

Plants are easy to accept. Here, for example, beside my deck, there is a humble little plant called a coyote bush. It is a small-leafed, scrubby, survivor-of-a-thing that hunkers low on sea-facing hillsides and consorts with mobs of blackberry brambles, forming dense, impenetrable thickets. Now, in spring, it looks like nothing. But in October—the hot, spare month when nothing seems to be blooming—suddenly, one afternoon, the sun will move in behind it, firing up the little furry flowers and setting the bush into a visual blaze. I can easily love this bush—not for its fruits, for it has none. Not for its rampant, high-colored blossoms, for it has none. Not for its shade, nor its graceful branches, and not for its mythological connotations, for it has none of these. But because I have seen, in that sunlit moment, its one glory.

Another thing about plants is that they let you practice—and fail—at commitment without felonious consequences. You leave a faithful schefflera in a house on another coast, and it grieves—some new renter may sear it in too much sun or drown it in overzealous watering—but its collapse is not something you will build your life around preventing. The plant is free to live or die. At home, you may surround yourself with cheery things in pots and then forget all about them when you go into a decline. No matter. They're used to the moods of nature, and while they might wither in protest or even die, you will not be arrested. Plants are willing, like certain qualities in the soul, to come back when you are ready. And if they don't, you can forget them, as you never can forget the person who did not call, who did not write.

Plants can teach tolerance. Think of the tiniest ones, the white ones that come up like stars on the floors of the Eastern spring woods or the gentle violets that poke through cracks in your neighborhood's sidewalks. You would not insult their innocent faces by calling their colors inadequate, suggesting they didn't make you happy, or saying, "you should be more like the flowers in California!" Never.

And here is the big one: Plants are not you. You do not mistake your inadequacies for theirs. They are what they are. You are not inclined to berate them for not pleasing you more, for they are only what they are. Above all, you don't lay your life's hopes on them and feel that through your perseverance, the coyote bush, say, will become a rose.

Loving plants is natural. So much easier than loving people, with their faults. I think of my beloved, breathing heavily in the night, close to my ear, so I cannot hear the wolf howl from across the mesa. Him, with his sneezes so loud they buckle the walls and scare the birds out of the bushes in the garden. Him, with his notebooks on topics from A to Z. Him, the one who speaks, but never listens.

As I tend its tough green leaves, remembering the brilliant blossoms on my dormant phalenopsis, I think of my beloved, filling the doorway, holding out roses. I think of the way he cocks his head and smiles when he says I look nice, the way he looks, by the fire, quiet for once, curled over his drawing, as he might have as a child of six. So innocent. But so complex. I smile. Start with plants? If he were a plant, he'd be a jungle.

How We Started

It began one summer afternoon, shortly after I moved here, when the phone rang. I was in my one-room rented studio by the sea, my refuge from my complicated east coast life. That day, I was happy. Sorting through some new negatives on my minilight table. Work was going well. I was not "looking for anyone." But when the phone rang, oddly, I knew it would be him—the tall, blonde English guy who was part of a group I'd met with the week before. They were working up a new kind of tech/art company. Someone in the group had seen my "reel" and thought they might like to have a photographer involved. I was curious, so I went. The English guy, the conceptual artist of the group, was fresh from London and wore a wheat-colored linen jacket, cerulean-blue shirt, and a tie with Picasso's *Les Demoiselles d'Avignon* parading naked down the front. Made me smile. He had an open, friendly face and a certain radiance about him. On the phone, he said he was in the area and that he'd like to talk some more about the company, what they were thinking, what they might need. I wasn't looking for work, but I was mildly intrigued. I said, "Sure, come to my place. I'll give you tea."

About twenty minutes later, we were sitting out on my patio overlooking the garden, with the blue horizon and San Francisco in the distance, and I was pouring him a nice cup of tea.

"Is it okay?" I asked him. "It's English Breakfast."

"Not bad, for an American," he said, with a sly smile. We talked about what we were each doing here, on this wild, woolly, west coast, so far from our respective city lives. He talked about the high-tech project that he and his group were forming, something with an "eco" emphasis, that he thought could use some fine art landscape photography and maybe video work. It sounded a little vague, and I was interested, but not in going back into a life of high stress production work. I told him I'd left that behind. He seemed to understand.

"You're a fine artist. We all saw it," he said. I asked if he'd like some more tea. We talked and laughed and laughed and talked. Then, as a fog started rolling in, I remembered myself and made the social gesture, standing up, clearing the plates, saying that nice as it was talking, I had plans. The light was good, it was time for me to take my camera to a place I'd been watching on the beach.

"Can I come too?"

"Well..." He had a really winning smile. "Okay." I took the dishes inside and got my gear. He asked if he could carry my tripod. This was probably, as we have since always laughed about, the gesture that won my heart.

Down on the beach, the scene was dramatic, as any Pacific coast scene is at just about any time. Cool, fog, gritty feeling on your face. Wind. I remember thinking how all this wind was terrible for the looks of my hair and then thinking, *oh, stop that. So what?* He was talking on animatedly about liveliness in my photographs, how some art is dead, but mine is so alive. He stopped talking while I worked, setting up the tripod, screwing on the field camera, pulling out the bellows, unwrapping the lens and slipping it into place, getting out my film plates, already loaded, and then, pulling out the dark cloth, whipping it around like a cape, draping it in around the camera like a hood and then huddling under it. With my head under the black cloth, all I could see was black and the glowing ground glass and the image, upside down, of him, hamming it up in front of me.

"Get out of the way! I'm looking at that driftwood!"

He stuck his face at the lens and, grinning, stepped away. In the quiet dark, I did my focusing and adjusting, and my nervousness settled down as it became just me and that upside-down image of the tortured form in the setting sun. When the graphics looked right, I reached into my bag for a film plate, slid it into the back, made the exposure. One, then another at a slightly wider aperture, just to be sure. And that was it. "All done!" The whole procedure took about twenty minutes. He spent the minutes sitting happily on a big eucalyptus log, watching the sun go down.

As we walked back up the crude steps that a local had carved into the hillside to ease the climb up to "the mesa," as it was called—the flat land that rose above the town as a sort of plateau—the English gentleman, carrier of my tripod, suggested we go get some dinner in town. I was starving. So I said, "Sure."

What happened next lives on in our house as a touchstone. When things get rough, he'll say, as he did just the other night when I was getting really depressed about our prospects, "Remember the hole?"

The hole. This man, who sees the metaphoric significance in things, reminds me of *the hole* almost every day now. And when I start going on about *what we are going to do?* and just before he starts storming around in frustration, he begs me to *remember the hole.*

It happened like this. At the end of the evening, we were chilly and tired, and I was hungry and delighted and looking forward to a lovely dinner in the restaurant in town with this amiable man. We reached the car, laughing and talking about what we would love to eat. They did a nice lamb kebab there. Or maybe a pizza? We dusted the sand off our shoes. I put my camera gear in the trunk and then climbed in the front of his great, gray Lexus. Anyone could see that this car was his pride and joy—the plush interior, the clean lines, and, waving out the back window, the little Union Jack flag on a stick. We were happily jouncing toward town down the deeply rutted dirt road when suddenly the Lexus lurched to a halt. What? We burst out of our doors. The right front end had plunged down into a hole, causing the rear end to lift, leaving the left wheel raised, as in a yoga pose, and spinning freely in the air.

"That doesn't look good," I said.

"Bugger," he said. Seeing the plight of his darling car, he started walking around, flapping his arms and raving. "What is this? We're in the middle of the bloody road! What kind of place is it where you can't drive in the middle of the bloody *road* without losing your bloody *car*?"

"The kind of place where people come to lose themselves," I said, wryly. He gave me a sort of politely scornful look—very British—then went on pacing and muttering about the idiocy of America and the road maintenance department.

Road maintenance department? Here? Where potholes were valued as features to keep cars going slow?

"But Robert," said I, ever the reasonable, "look around! We're in the middle of a dirt road in the middle of nowhere! There is no road maintenance department."

Not to mention we were an hour's drive from any Triple A rescue. Bugger indeed. Now I really was getting hungry. He was getting more and more indignant. The sun was sinking, along with our spirits. Wind combed through the now gray grasses in the field alongside us.

"Well. That's no excuse. There should be," he said, still grumbling and huffing about the mythical maintenance department.

I paced around behind him, worried that the café in town would close and how I'd now have to go to bed without dinner.

Then, out of the blue, he stopped pacing.

"Wait," he said. "This reminds me of something."

"What?" I said, starting to feel tired.

"This hole."

"What about it?"

"Look at it." He faced me, eyes bright, hands open as if holding a watermelon. "We met. We went down this hole. And now we're going to get out of it! We're looking at our future!"

And he was happy about this?

All I knew was that we needed to get to a phone and to the café. I led us toward a house that had some lights on. He followed, talking, getting cheerier every moment.

"We're not out yet," I said, somewhat irritated.

"Just wait. This will mark our whole life together. You'll see."

We reached the house, a low, white frame house surrounded by overgrown bushes. No dogs barked. Knocked at the door. A sky-blue door freshly painted. The woman who answered the door, an older woman with long white hair, fringed jeans, and flowered shirt, heard our story and right away called her friend the fire chief. And sure enough, within the half hour, a shiny tow truck arrived and pulled us out of the hole. After a lot of back-slapping and shaking hands on the part of Robert and his new best friend, we were finally back in the Lexus, which had suffered no structural damage that we could see. So we were on our way. But not, alas, to the restaurant, which was, by then, closed.

"We've missed the café," I said, rather wanly, as the fire chief chugged away, and we swayed and clung to our seats as the Lexus surfed the rutted dirt road toward town.

"Well, we could always go to my place."

Amazingly enough, this savvy Londoner had decided to rent a little cabin out here, near one of his colleagues, and to be near to the ocean. Nice change from London, he explained. I *bet*, I thought.

"My landlady's away," he said. "We can make something to eat there." I shot him a questioning look.

"It's cool," he said, with a cheery grin.

By now it was dark. I didn't know the area, but after a few U-turns and down a long road, he pulled the car to a stop and we got out. The air was full of the tangy smell of eucalyptus and pine. Tiny little wind chimes were tinkling in the mist. I followed him down a wooden walkway onto a porch and into a house, which, he told me, was just a few yards away from the cabin he was renting. This was a whole new experience, I thought, going along, ready for anything. Inside the house, he flicked on a light, and I found myself in a kitchen, staring at a row of suspended pots and pans. His landlady, he said again, wouldn't mind if we made ourselves something to eat.

It was odd to be rummaging around in a strange kitchen with a strange man in a strange house that belonged to someone I'd never met. But with the café in town closed, we were lucky to be able to forage for something to turn into a meal. The whole experience was disorienting.

Every kitchen speaks its own language. Some kitchens, you walk in and understand every word: You want an onion, "Here I am!" You want a corkscrew, "Here I am!" It all makes sense. This hand-crafted, open-beamed redwood kitchen made no sense to a person used to conventional, Eastern architecture. Where there should be knives and forks, there were potholders. Where there should be glasses, there were plates. Where there should be a garbage bag, there was a vacuum cleaner. On and on. Illogical. I wondered: *is this how Californians think?*

Little by little, as the tall man talked, his words lilting easy and unendingly off a northern English tongue, I got a kind of dinner going. I'm good at making dinners out of nothing, but I'm not good at figuring out what's going on between two people. The conversation—originally about the company he and his colleagues were putting together—kept slipping off the track. Was this a business meeting or a date? Who knew? I thought: *now where would she keep the salt?*

When the meal was assembled, I took our plates to the table. Lit candles. He sat at one end, I sat at the other. The food went down without much comment. I wondered about him. Was he wondering about me? Did he think me attractive? Did I need another distraction? As we finished and I cleared the plates and moved to take them to the kitchen, he rose, took the plates, set them down, reached for me.

We were standing at the kitchen counter. I remember his breath. His warmth. I remember his talking about myths of the Underworld and that hole back in the road while my body was having a wholly different experience. His body, almost a foot taller than mine, had a just-right feel. His graceful slightness felt non-threatening, easy. Every part of me he touched, as he drew me to him, warmed me. His kiss, which I did not resist, ignited nearly forgotten energies, and we moved together in the flow of those energies to the door.

I followed him into the night, down the long wooden walkway to his cabin, my sandals slapping on the hollow-sounding boards. Many tiny wind chimes were pinging the air like fairy bells. The autumn air was black, crisp. A little white Halloween ghost fluttered around the light over his landlady's door, going *Whooooo, Wooooooo*. Then his hand on the back of my jacket. Then the dark and warm, man-smelling cabin. Then the heat of his skin.

3

The Decision

It was a month before the wedding. I was in New York, visiting my mother. It was snowing. I'd just hung up the phone. My mother sat opposite me at the table by the window. Midtown was nothing but whiteness. Silence. No cab horses' clop-clopping. No chorus of taxi horns. No shouts or screams. The usual nighttime sounds and lights were muffled in soft, drifting snow. The coolness was quite unlike the fever in my head after the phone call. I was crying. My mother poured a glass of wine and pushed it gently toward me.

"Are you sure you want this?" She didn't mean the wine.

"This," was the Englishman, my beloved, on the other end of the line, now four time zones away, who had been yelling at me. We were to be signing a contract on a house of our own as soon as the wedding was done. Our own house on the California coast. My dream. A continent away from Midtown and all it implied of my former life, and an ocean away from London and all it implied of his. Yes. I wanted this. The house, him, all of it. Just not these arguments.

This argument, that had me in tears and had just terminated in a slammed down phone, was not new. We seemed to be having arguments all the time. They were like tropical storms. When they were over, and all was sunny, I never could say what they were about. Stupid things, little things. It didn't matter. They were never logical. They were like sudden explosions in a peaceful pasture long ago planted with mines. They were like force fields interacting. They were like the proverbial briar patch from which, once ventured into, one cannot exit unscathed. Sometimes, desperate to have the bellowing end, I would grab the car keys and go for the door. Then he'd grab his and try to get out ahead of me, and we'd block each other in the doorway. "You can't go, I'm going!" And I'd yell back, "No! You can't go, I'm going!" Then, we'd end up wrestling and laughing and then race each other to the car to drive into town for some pie.

But this one was different. There was no wrestling into laughter, no friendly pie. Just the cold logic of our voices on opposite ends of the phone, his biting anxiety, and my near hysteria. Why?

As I explained to my mother after he so unceremoniously hung up, I'd simply said that I was anxious about having no space of my own once we were married. That I would need my space. I thought that was a perfectly reasonable concern. But Bam! He blew up. "Why are we even getting married, then?"

I tried to explain, but he kept screaming, bloody hell this and bugger that, and then about how he needed to be heard. When I finally screamed back, "But I need to be heard too!" he hung up.

So. There I was, sitting at a small table in front of a second-floor window in the heart of Midtown, with snow sifting innocently down, and my mother sitting opposite in her silk wrapper, with her little wine glass, looking so nice and so normal, while my whole life was spinning out of control.

After taking a sip of wine—a Napa Valley cab she had brought up from the store downstairs—my mother sighed. Hers was the rueful sigh of a desirable woman in her sixties, who long ago decided she preferred to live alone, to focus on her career and her work, rather than suffer the moods and needs of a difficult husband. "You may have to let him go," she said simply. "You don't want to make the same mistake again."

She never shot an arrow without hitting the bull's eye.

Was this a mistake?

When my mother got up from the table to check on dinner, I called my best friend, down in Washington. I said, "I can't do it."

"Can't do what?"

"I can't go through with it. It's impossible! When every little thing has to explode into one of these arguments?"

"He loves you."

"I know," I said, and stopped crying. "I love him too. But I won't survive in a house with a man who needs to argue me to the ground over every little thing. I won't survive it."

"I know," she said. "But remember Virginia Woolf? Every creative woman needs a room of her own?"

"Hell with that, I need a building of my own!"

The sentence hung there, a simple truth, like a clothesline full of happy washing, the words like little dresses flapping freely in the sunlight. We started to laugh. Yes. To be married—to this man, to any man—I need—we all need—a building of our own. Yes! Yes, that is the way for a creative woman to survive a marriage. Now, how to do it.

My friend and I plotted out a plan I could live with. Then, full of resolve, I composed myself and called him back. I explained that I loved him and wanted the best for us both. He, the man who had been such a pounder, reverted immediately to his better self and was soft and loving and cautiously amenable to the deal I carefully proposed. Which was this: We would proceed with the wedding and the house, as planned. And yes, I can provide—through my own resources—a building of my own. Very small. No frills. Just a little building, on the property we will share, that will be my place of work, that will be mine and mine alone. At core, a fair and kind man, he understood. As an artist too, he got it. He supported my creativity and wanted my happiness. As I wanted his. I went over our understanding about my little building very carefully.

"And no one will be able to visit there unless invited."

"Well, I can go there, as your husband."

"No. No one."

"But what if there's an emergency?"

"Like what kind of emergency?" I was puzzled at the thought.

"What if I need to ask you a question." Ha.

"You can wait."

"But what if we need some milk?" Really!

Here, I must pause. There are certain dynamics that women who have children will instantly recognize, either with humor or frustration. The sweet delight of their child's insistent need. And the horror, when that need is frustrated, of the child's rage. I had not then, nor in the future, thought about having children, and so I missed the profound education that relationship can provide. I was unequipped to recognize sweet need in the outbursts of the fully grown man. I saw only the rage when his need was frustrated. When I met that rage in kind, as I often did in the early days, everything exploded. On the rare times when I was at my best, I dealt the rage or the outburst with patience and reason. Lucky for me, I was at my best discussing the rules around my little building. Yes, he could call in case of emergency. And if we ran out of milk he could go to town and get some. That hurdle surmounted, our plans moved forward.

A Building of One's Own

Our contractor, Antonio, who was making some improvements on the house, agreed that when the work we'd planned to do inside the house—a darkroom for me, an office for him—was complete, he could erect a 10-by-10 "garden shed" (the only other structure the county would allow on the property) as my writing retreat. It would have redwood siding and deck, a salt-box roof, sliding glass door on one side, long "pop-out" window and window seat facing the meadow, regular window on the opposite side facing east, and one wall of bookshelves and wraparound desk. Nice bare pine floor. Facing away from the house, the building would be surrounded by meadow, blackberries, and woods and a view of the western sky. It was to be utterly private. My deck and little clearing in front would be open to animals and birds. A little *Casita*, as Antonio called it. And so, it was named.

Building the Casita was the outward manifestation of the inner process of creating my own ground in the new marriage. I'd failed at marriage before and wanted to succeed this time, to be "together" without losing my "self." Was that possible? Ideally, the little building would shelter and contain that effort.

The ground I sought, in life and art, was based in the land. Nature. I wanted to be surrounded by all the living expressions of the Earth, to be present, and to respond. For a model of purpose, the cabin of Thoreau was eloquent. Minimal, stripped down to basics, his retreat to the pond allowed his senses to open to all of Nature's messaging. His intention, I discovered when reading *Walden*, was in line with my own. He wrote: "I went to the woods because I wished to live deliberately, to front only the essential facts of life, and see if I could not learn what it had to teach, and not, when I came to die, discover that I had not lived."

His form was an extreme and unattainable model for the city likes of me—who went up to the house for meals and to the store for provisions—but the intention was similar, and so he became a soul companion of a sort in my effort. Ideally, the little building would shelter and contain that effort. My Casita was not rough-hewn like his cabin but was nevertheless spare, focused, and intimate with the land. Within its walls, I would be alone, in communion with and surrounded by nature and—for I am not a true recluse—a mere fifty yards from the warmth of home, hearth, and my beloved. Ideal.

The process of building the Casita began, as all creative projects do, with clearing the space. We all—me, Robert, and Antonio—worked on this part together. Clearing space for the building was hard. But for me, not as hard as learning to work with "the boys." This came into focus after we had been hacking all day into the impenetrable tangle of blackberry and poison oak that is the native ground cover around here. By the time the light was starting to slant, we'd leveled a square about 20 by 20 and were tired. As we rested on our tools, my eye fell upon a little sapling, a mere four feet into the brush. I said, "I'm going to free that tree." The boys both said, "Count us out, we're done." They lay down their machetes and weed whackers and shears and shovels and reached into the cooler and popped open beers. The hapless little sapling, arms outstretched, was begging, "Free me!" I could hear it. I went forward with machete and sickle and conviction. When I finally cut it free, the little sapling looked spindly and weak, like a leg released from a cast. I said to Antonio, "I think it's a fruit tree." He said, "No. It's not a fruit tree." But as I hacked away and studied its leaves, I was sure, well almost sure, that it was some kind of fruit tree, maybe even an apple. Time would tell.

When the clearing was done, Antonio put in the footings and framed up the walls. With all of us helping, one side went up, then another, then the others. The windows went in. The sliding glass door. Insulation in the ceiling. Then, the dry wall. I learned to spackle. Loved to spackle. Then, the roof. I learned to tack in roof tiles. Hated tacking in roof tiles. Gruesome job. But, like mountain climbing, which I did but once and found it grueling, I loved that I did it. The little building was sealed in my sweat.

The detailing inside the Casita was simple. The place was only 10 by 10, with a three-foot "pop out." So, it had to be economical with space. Think of a boat. The place where I sat, at my little Mac SE, was opposite the window seat, and had a double-hung window through which I could sit and watch the rising sun through the big pines up by the road. All around me, I'd installed a "core" selection of books, my collection of rocks from Maine, various bones and feathers brought up from our beach. Opposite the wall of books, I had a white, muslin curtain mounted on a wooden pole over the sliding glass door. Outside on the tiny deck, I had one redwood chair. In the cleared patch below the deck, I put in a big leathery gunnera plant, some herbs and grasses, and a birdbath. It was a bit of a walk from the house, and my privacy was secured. The mysteries of happiness expanded.

One mystery about a building of one's own is that, as a sanctuary, especially when hard won, just knowing it is there has a calming effect. The ritual of making morning coffee, up early in the quiet house, then taking the short walk from the house, down the path to the Casita, became a transition from the complexity of being "together," to the peace of simply being. That this serenity of being was anchored by the presence of the man, up in the main house, was both a mystery and a challenge.

4

A Solitude of Two

Robert and I have a joke between us that started when I agreed we could marry. "If we must be one, can it be me?" said I, and we both laughed. This oneness within separateness—or separateness within oneness—that marriage requires is very hard to imagine, much less manage.

This morning, at the Sunday morning talk in the Zen Center in the redwoods down the coast, the monk spoke about the source of all evil and suffering having to do with our feeling of separateness from others, which comes with a feeling of loneliness and alienation. Who hasn't felt that? Spiritual awareness, however, shows us that we are all part of one whole—as nature is one and one is all. To reconcile the difference between the separateness we feel and the consciousness or oneness we might achieve, he offered a helpful image. He called it the upright position. In this position, you do not lean forward, you do not lean back, you do not lean to the right or to the left. You are upright. You are in balance. You are ready. Not just for attack, as in a martial arts practice, or for an embrace, as in love, but for all and everything. Adopting this stance, he admitted, is not simple.

"Try it," said the monk. "You cannot maintain the upright position for an hour. You cannot even hold it for a second. In other words, it is an aim." Something to imagine. A way to stand as you regard yourself and the world. How to find that place to stand?

"So," the monk said, "from the upright position, you may observe, say, that your intimate one—the one you feel to be as one with you, the extension of yourself—may be doing something in a way that you would not do. Perhaps you are in a car, and he or she is making turns you know to be wrong or taking directions you know to be inefficient. You possibly become irritated." Titters and chuckles of recognition wafted around the Zendo.

I was tittering too. I know that wrong turn well. That not starting up at the light fast enough, or starting too fast, or ten thousand other things that will trigger a blast of English correction from my beloved, which will then trigger a very American response from me, which will cause the whole exchange to escalate. And so, I pay attention to the monk's words. He says what makes amazingly perfect sense but is still mysterious: "You suddenly realize he or she is separate from you, and this produces pain. The more you can stay in awareness of that basic pain, and not evade it or grow numb to it, the more you are in touch with the basic pain of existence."

The monk knows this is difficult. He is simply giving us the lessons. Receiving the lesson is not a solution; it's simply an acknowledgment of what you have been given. But if you take it onboard, the lesson can be the beginning of a practice. A practice is not a solution either, as it will consist of continual and repeated failure. So what am I doing? What am I hoping for? I am hoping to learn to see, through the multiple irritations of life and togetherness, with clarity. For myself, and my beloved.

The Practice of Paying Attention

The practice of mindfulness, like the practice of artmaking, puts one constantly at war with comfort. Always the questions: Why are you doing this? What is the point? Who really cares? Why does it matter? And wouldn't I rather be taking a nap? Yes, I want to remember every blade of grass in this place I love, should I have to leave it. Yes, I am making my photographs to capture each movement of light over the land. Yes, I am breathing and listening and watching. Yes, I want to experience every moment I have here and will preserve as many as I can in silver, in the darkroom. So?

But is that like putting all your silver in a knapsack as you're fleeing a flood? When the Zen monks talk of letting go, am I doing the opposite?

This morning I opened a much loved, faded blue, cloth-bound book, *The Phenomenon of Man*, by Pierre Teilhard de Chardin, the Jesuit priest and paleontologist, published in 1955, the year of his death. The book has been with me since I was twenty and is on the shelf beside me now in the Casita. wI was given it by an artist boyfriend when I was just peeking into the outside world of adulthood to see where I'd fit. I have not opened the book for a long time. Now, when I turn the slightly yellowed pages, I find underlined words in the Foreword, which is entitled "Seeing." Here he says, "The history of the living world can be summarized as the elaboration of ever more perfect eyes within a cosmos in which there is always something more to be seen."

When I first read this, I imagined a universe alive in some way that is not how we normally think of it, rather in some more essential way. It seemed to me that Teilhard imagines a whole creative, generative phenomenon that, he says, reflects itself in my seeing. That I am part of it and that somehow my seeing matters. "The work of human works," he writes, "is to establish, in and by means of each one of us, an absolutely original center in which the universe reflects itself in a unique and inimitable way."

That my seeing may in some way enhance something larger than myself is a concept I've had inklings of along the way. I remember once, basking in the sun out on some elephantine rocks along a quiet cove in Maine, a photographer friend and I were admiring clouds. He was known for his clouds and landscapes that spoke of a presence beyond the mundane. In some of his prints, I could almost hear the forms murmuring. We were sharing a deli lunch of cheese sandwiches and bottled water, and he was talking about the beauty of creation. "He needs our help," he said, without naming what I assumed he would mean the Creator or, in a more secular way, the Universe. He was a master. I did not question. He introduced me to the poetry of Rainer Maria Rilke, who also refers to this need of something outside of ourselves, for our vision. In the "First Duino Elegy," Rilke wrote,

> *Yes, the springtimes needed you. Often a star*
> *was waiting for you to notice it. A wave rolled toward you*
> *out of the distant past, or as you walked*
> *under an open window, a violin*
> *yielded itself to your hearing. All this was mission.*

This, in my own humble realm, is my daily place of beginning. A practice. Right now, instead of stepping out onto the deck and going quickly down the path to my Casita as I do every morning, I step out onto the deck and stop. And listen for the low, distant, roar of the ocean. Then, nearby, in the bushes, the twitter of little birds. All around, the atmosphere is morning gray and the whisper-cool mist on my face is spicy, with the complex scent of earth, eucalyptus, and salt. Surrounding me are all the living forms that, along with weather and plate tectonics and my many gardening mistakes, create the character of this place. Living plants. Many times, in a given day, I walk by them, on the way to or from, this or that, and only halfway acknowledge them in the swish of my haste. Today I want to stop, breathe, and take them in.

Imagine that in the composition of a place, plants are like the letters in a word. Groupings in the garden are like the words in a paragraph, essential, defining, full of color, tone, desire, and information. How often I am guilty of speed-reading past them, trying in my mind to get to some major meaning, trying to get to the "what should be" or "what might be," and all the time, walking by the simple what is. Not today.

Today, right in front of my eyes, with the glow of the new sun faintly burning through the mist, right here, embracing the front of the deck, I acknowledge the spicy green mass of the rockrose (*Cistus*). This tough old bush has been hugging the deck since the house was built, some ten years before we found it. Right now, it is sleeping, its stiff little leaves as gray-green as the mist. By May, the whole bush will be dotted in five-petal blossoms the size of cocktail umbrellas, pink and fragile as if made from fine rice paper. At the base of each petal is a dark red spot, as if a painter had given a dab of color to accentuate the small yellow pistil that rises in the center. Bees love the rockrose, and in the spring and summer, they will be buzzing and diving and rummaging in the pinkness of the flowers. The black-tailed deer, who love roses, walk right by the rockrose, favoring the standard roses I have given up trying to grow. Members of the deer population consider the Coat of Many Colors, and the Pristine and the Blaze roses to be delicacies, and carefully, with their soft muzzles pluck the whole rose off the branch without getting stuck by the thorns. The deer are well-adapted specialists, and they routinely, often severely, sometimes tragically, as when a newly planted fruit tree is nibbled to death, edit my garden design. But they leave the rockrose alone, so that when nothing else is blooming, I can always pick a sweet pink sprig for the table.

By the stairs of the deck sprawls the almost out-of-control, spreading-everywhere Rosemary bush. I can cut it forever, put it in chicken, in vases, in sachets, and never run out of it. Nothing eats it. But in the spring, it has tiny blue blossoms that the bees, when they're tired of rockrose, descend upon and savor. Sometimes when climbing the few steps up to the deck, the buzzing can awaken one if nothing else does.

Out on the path, sheltering the driveway from the road, is the stately, exotic *Echium candicans* (Pride of Madeira). Originally from North Africa, the *Echium* is a particularly California-looking plant, with big dry-sticky, blue-green leaves and great, audacious blue flowered spikes that reach for the sky throughout the warmer months. The multitude of little blue florets that cover the spikes are usually humming, like the rockrose and the Rosemary, with bees. In the autumn, the *Echium* is a blue paradise for the newly arrived orange Monarchs, creating a pattern of color that dizzies the eyes. To me, it is both a glory and a mystery.

The *Echium* seems to grow almost anywhere, providing there is sun. Here in my garden, the *Echium* grows strong and luxuriant. But—at least in my experience—should you try to move a new shoot with the idea that it would be better over there, or there, or somewhere it does not prefer, you will come out in the morning and face a plant that looks as if it's been sucking on lemons. From there, it's all downhill. When you transplant an *Echium*—or at least when I transplant one—it just dies. However, should a hole appear in a border, as happens up by the road from time to time, say, when an *Acacia* or something else gives out, then magically, and of its own accord, a new *Echium* plant will grow up and fill it in instantly. They just want to do it on their own, thank you.

Stepping down onto the path on the way to the Casita, looking to the left, my eye follows the crease in the land where the downward slope from my property meets the upward slope from the opposite property. In that fold, in the winter, runs a little swale, a place of tall grasses and seasonal rainwater. Today, the deep greens of the grass are shocked by a sudden burst of whiteness. Calla lilies!

Calla lily clusters live wild in this area, loving the swampy places by the lagoon and places in land where water collects. They are said to start blooming in May. But here it is still March! And there they are—a clutch of them blooming, way ahead of schedule, even as chill rains still threaten. This is a land of surprises.

Beside the birdbath in front of the deck this morning, the kaffir lily has sent up a bud that is swelling and ready to pop open. Another surprise. This kaffir, spring's first dainty step, is a lily of hope. We bought it one day last August on one of our Sunday drives up the north coast, where we liked to stop for romantic outdoor lunches and leisurely walks on the beach. This drive was different. The fawned-over Lexus had been sold to cover expenses, and we were driving a hand-me-down Volvo, and we declined both wine and dessert when we stopped for lunch. Afterwards, when we visited the nursery, as I always liked to do, we vowed for once not to buy. But it's easier to resist dessert than a blossoming plant, and I longed for the salmon-red lily. I looked up at my dear husband, the generous English gentleman, who can refuse me nothing. He smiled. It's only three dollars. He pulled out his wallet, took out his last three bills and said I should have it, because it is beautiful. I hugged him. I felt guilty but glad. The lily was mine and what a beauty. Kaffir lily. I even loved the name. When we got home, I decided to plant it in a prominent spot, symbolic of my new favorite theme: Spending as an act of faith.

If spending is an act of faith, then planting trees is an act of hope. In the early days, as we were settling into our life here, whenever I became anxious about money, I planted a tree. Oh, sure, I could have spent the money on a meal, or a haircut, or applied it to an invoice, but all those things relate to real money, whereas the fifty dollars, presented in the form of plastic, is but a wish. And a wish should be planted, not spent.

I look around. Times must have been hard for a while, for I have lots of trees. The little pink flowering plum, for example, up by the drive, with the three open blooms, I bought one day in the pouring rain two years ago when my faith in our prospects was beginning to waver. Ninety-nine dollars. My last $100 bill from my secret savings.

At home, I went out in the rain, dug a big hole, and the tree went in and settled in the muck and stood straight and faced right, and I felt that if the tree could look so brave in all this rain, then I could too. Those ninety-nine dollars have compounded many times over in pleasure. Each spring, the little tree is the first in my garden to bloom and reminds me that winter—and other hard times—will pass.

5

Narrative Wilderness

The real estate man rang this morning to say he had a couple from the city who may be interested in the house and suggested, in a spirit of optimism—the market was "pretty bad"—that we might do some prettying up of the garden before he brought them around. Sure. Sure.

I confess to being only moderately enthusiastic about "prettying up" the place, as we do for some strangers to tramp through, tapping their clipboards. But when it comes to the garden, I am resistant, bordering on irate.

First, I should say that when I use the term "garden," I will admit to exaggeration. When we first moved in, a landscape architect friend sent us a beautiful book about California gardens. Looking through it, without my glasses, my eye caught a pleasing phrase: "Narrative Wilderness." Yes! Exactly! That's what I've got here! A narrative wilderness. A tangled mass of plants and animals, stories, and images, hopes, and disappointments. Each of the plants and animals and birds here thrives as much in spite of me as because of me. Each has its originating nature, and, thanks to me, each participates in a story. Which is what I thought the phrase "narrative wilderness" was about.

The writer of the genuine garden book, of course, never heard of the phrase to which I'd taken such a fancy. She—my glasses later revealed—was talking about *"native wilderness"* and had in mind, being of California, the sort of benevolent tangle that thrived here before people started messing with it. The idea was that flora and fauna that originate in a place, or have become long habituated to it, learn to manage the challenges local to the area. Other species, brought in from elsewhere... not so good.

Bamboo, for example. Neighbors warned me that it was nonnative to California. It will take over, they said. I'll be sorry. Pretty as they are now, they'll push out everything else. Find something native, they said. I listened to their advice and planted it anyway, beside the deck of my Casita. I love the airiness of bamboo, and the sound it makes in the wind, and the way the leaves hold and play with sunlight. So I am ready to help my beautiful bamboo establish themselves here in harmony—with pruning shears and shovel if necessary.

The bird of paradise is another story. It has a tropical beauty, seen in hotels in Los Angeles, with a long, full bud like a heron's beak. To have planted this exotic figure amongst my common grasses was a fantasy fulfilled. But to be truthful, when the bloom arrived, it was a little out of place. It should be poised against a sun-blasted stucco-white wall, bathed in white L.A. light, not stuck in the fog against faded redwood siding on this weather-beaten coast.

Still, some nonnatives simply make the place. Like the yellow acacias, those wild Australian bushes that will grow house high in a couple of years and then, in a storm or from exhaustion or just a bad air day, will suddenly say, "That's it. I'm done," and collapse from within. Mine, up by the road, given a few sunny days, will be ready to burst into bloom. Soon, the whole southerly boundary of our property will be a billowing sea of yellow.

Soon after the acacias burst into bloom, the beautiful, deadly, white *Datura* that now drapes itself over my back fence, looking as tired as we feel, will unfurl its heavy, trumpetlike flowers that will drip from its limbs like a sorrow. The bloom exudes a tropical odor and is reported to have psychedelic powers. Like a bad romance, it can poison the brain. It was outlawed in Florida after some kids died having done whatever they did with the flower to get high.

The *Datura* plant was given to me as a "new house" present by a neighbor. Hilda, a gruff-voiced Polish woman who long ago fled Hitler's invasion, lived next door to the studio I rented when I first came here. Hilda was always yelling at something. I could hear her at all hours, calling into the mist, "Coconut! Coconut! Get in heeah!" Coconut was her waddling, aged sheepdog who had been sleeping, sound as a stone, somewhere just down the hill under the Monterey pine. He'd rouse himself and, stiff-legged, tail-wagging low, come up to the house to his old friend, who'd keep yelling until the dog was inside. The woman, with long, white hair falling to her shoulders, was probably in her seventies, but didn't seem to know it. Like a flower child from another day, she wore wild hand-tie-dyed colors and erected, all over her copiously flowering garden, sexually explicit, energetic sculptures of Pan and goats that she fashioned out of driftwood dragged up from the beach. She tolerated few people but seemed to like me and was fond of giving me plants. "Be careful of this one," she said last summer, as she handed me the outrageously languorous *Datura* in a fistful of soil. "Even I wouldn't try them!" *Haw haw haw. Daturas.* So beautiful. So deadly. And now, right at home on my back fence. When it blooms, it reminds me: time is deadly; now is beautiful. Careful what you inhale!

On the front deck, just after the acacia blooms, the aphrodisiacal jasmine, that reaches from the planter to the roof, will be buzzing with bees, its blossoms filling the mornings with perfume. This is a moment I wait for. On the day we moved in, my beloved presented the plant to me in a small pot surrounded by pink foil with a pink ribbon as a welcome to us. I tucked it in the planter on the deck right away, nurtured it and fussed over it. Each year I proclaim how well it's growing and how happy it is in its place, implying that the same goes for ourselves.

To some new owner, my jasmine will have no such history. It will be simply a plant, maybe too rangy, maybe needing pruning, maybe just not fitting in their idea of deck decor. It will be stripped of the meaning it enjoys as part of our history. The idea of leaving the jasmine I have loved and tended pulls at me and with it the perennial question: Do we tend things because we love them? Or do we love them because we tend them?

Or because they remind us, in some way, of ourselves?

The Refugee Gardener

A middle-aged widow who lives down the road from our house has an odd gardening habit. I've watched it evolve since I first came to this place and rented a studio on her property. The room for rent, as advertised, had privacy, a view of the sea, and a walk-in closet. Perfect. Who needs a kitchen? With the sea view and a sloping garden of sages and succulents rolling out from under a low, redwood deck, this room of my own was everything I could want in what was then a transition time. Sophie, the owner, was open and friendly. She had flashing black eyes, a trace of a middle European accent, and a wide, photogenic smile. In her flowered shawl and winter-heavy caftan, she had the kind of beauty that must have made her a slayer of men in her youth and, I suspected, attracted them to her even now.

As we discussed the possibilities of my renting the space—how I'd be back and forth from the East for a while till my project commitments were finished; how I was independent—no husband, no children, no hangers on; and how I was there to write and photograph—we were instantly compatible. I'd be a "light" renter. She'd be a harmonious landlady. I asked her why she was renting the space, and she admitted that she loved being in the room, looking out at her garden and the sea beyond, but it made sense to let someone else have it. By that, I took it to mean that she needed the cash. As for me, as I was "Goldilocks-ing" my way up the coast, looking to test out and find the just-right place to start a new life, I had plenty of cash, wanted the view, and wrote a check on the spot.

As I grew to know her on our walks on the beach after I moved in, I found her attractions and repulsions, the push-pull of her relationships, as she described them, to be fascinating. I think she shared her stories with me for my benefit as I was trying to restructure my own independent life. She seemed happy alone, as well as with men friends with whom she was close, but not too close. They all seemed to irritate her in one way or another: this one too needy, the other never around. She had many women friends whom she mentored and cared for, as she did her grown children, but whose faults, like those of her children, she also was keen to observe. From what I could see, what she loved with pure passion, without reservation, was the place where she lived.

When she saw I was home, she would invite me for tea on her deck or to walk with her to the beach or to join her in a hot tub, where we could watch the sunset over the ocean through a foreground of steam. On these walks, we would talk about our lives. She was interested in the media work I'd left back east, directing interviews with Holocaust survivors for an oral history project. I told her that after two years of going into the studio every day and listening to such soul-ripping stories, I'd had it. I had to leave. "When I signed the contract, they told me it would change my life," I said. "I didn't imagine how completely that was true." Since then, when faced with any decision, my answers always began with...if you have only one life...When I said that to her, she understood. She knew all about the Holocaust, she said, with a wry smile. As a young child in Poland, when things started looking bad for the Jews, she and her family had fled, settling briefly into interim sanctuaries until life became too dangerous, and they made a definitive escape to America. Many of her family were killed. She told me all this with studied lack of emotion, but there was a bite around the edges of her words—the way a hoar frost seems to bite the edges of winter morning leaves.

Listening to her story—the fleeing, settling in, fleeing, settling in, fleeing again—I began to sense a key to the garden mystery that had been gnawing at me since I met her, which looked like this:

Phase one. Sitting out on the deck, in the middle of a pleasant conversation about things we mutually enjoyed—food in San Francisco, ocean swimming here in October, whale-watching out near the Farallon Islands—or things we did not enjoy—tourists in the town, controlling behavior in males, what was happening in politics—suddenly, she would stop.

"Look. See that?"

She would point straight ahead to a place in her garden where a nice little plant would be growing contentedly, setting new leaves, enjoying the security of its roots, well situated even in the solid clay. Sophie, as if electrified, would stand up, frown, and, retrieving a shovel, march down the steps and into the garden, and dig up or yank out the little plant, and stuff it down—sometimes not even into a proper hole—somewhere else.

Phase two. As nature's creations do when deprived of home ground and sustenance, the disrupted plant would begin to wither and turn brown. After a couple of days, or by the next time I stopped in to visit, Sophie would look at it with puzzled disappointment and say, "I don't know if it's going to make it."

Phase three. One of two things would happen. Either the plant would continue to die a slow and pitiful death or, clutching its new piece of soil, would manage to suck some life from the earth and, if a plant could stagger, would stagger forward to life. In the first case, nothing is ever said about it. In the second case, she would say, in a triumphant voice, "See! It's going to make it!"

I watched this pattern, in bafflement, from the time I lived in her rental studio till just this past weekend, when a door of illumination flung open. I was walking on the path by her garden, and from over the fence, I saw her leaning on her shovel in a patch of sun. She was wearing a quilted red silk jacket over gray sweatpants stuffed into Cossack-looking boots, her short, straight graying-brown hair blowing across her clean, square jaw. She waved at me, smiling that triumphant smile. She pointed at two crocuses. "Look!" she said. "They made it!"

Crocuses. She had transplanted crocuses in midbloom—and they made it. In a moment of archetypal resonance, I saw her in her completeness. However much she had survived love and loss and grown into the independent woman I'd come to know, something about her must have remained locked in her early years, a child and young adult constantly uprooted, plunked down, threatened, and uprooted again. Deeply buried beneath her highly educated and graceful persona, some ghost of the Holocaust refugee remains, rises, and when she least expects it, acts out its dramas in her garden—the way an angry child might punish her dolls.

Seeing that, I now feel as sympathetic for her as I have been for her plants. Now, when I stop in to visit, I accept that her plants will be tortured and made to feel like orphans. I accept that she will celebrate those that survive and ignore the suffering others. Sometimes, when I'm visiting, I pick up her shovel, ask her permission, and gently, tenderly, replant the latest victim, nestling it easily into the earth, and giving it—and her—my understanding.

I never discuss this with her. Even now, we don't know each other that well. But, in my small way, I consider I am offering her a prayer. A tiny gesture of amends. No one, not even a plant, wants to be uprooted from home ground.

Freedom in Context

This morning comes in with the sound of the red-shouldered hawk. His two note cry opens a window in my mind, far back in time: I am in Virginia, feeling the warm earth-heat of a summer day rising from the floor of an unfamiliar woods. The blue-eyed cat that followed me belonged to the man I loved then, and we were on the way, the cat and I, down the baking lane, to the shelter of that man's house. Safety, newness, also fear of loss. The hawk's cry, then and now, stitching together two eras in my life.

The willow, which I see now from my bed in the house that is up for sale, fills the window. It waves at the sky with its soft shade of green. The hawk's call and that particular shade of green take me even further back in time, way before Virginia, to when I was little, in the fifties. My family—my parents, little sister, and I—lived in a brick colonial house similar to others in the new development just outside of Washington, D.C. The front yard had a sidewalk leading from the porch to the car at the curb, and the large back yard adjoined all the others. The whole development had been part of a grand old farm, of which no sign remained, except for one: In front of the house, in an area that separated our street from the street and houses that lay opposite, ran a little stream lined with great old willow trees. From our second-floor bedroom windows, I could look out and watch the willows sway in the wind.

My sister and I played in the stream. Nobody was afraid of Lyme disease then. Nobody was afraid of abduction. In the summers, we took our bikes and followed the stream down into a big pine wood where the stream widened. We also took our pets—the only pets that, after a long campaign, we'd succeeded in having our mother agree to. The campaign had consisted of intermittent begging until one day, out of the blue, she said, "Okay, girls. We'll go to the pet shop." We jumped up and down. We were five and seven. We knew we couldn't have a pony, though we yearned for one. But "A puppy! A puppy!"

"No," she said. "Not a puppy." *Awww. Well . . .*

"A kitten! A kitten!"

"No," she said patiently. *Awwwww.* We were genuinely puzzled. Then what?

"Girls," our mother said with dramatic largesse, "You can each have a turtle." She was being nice. We swallowed our disappointment, which transformed into delight when we held the small, cool creatures, straining, as we were, for life and adventure.

When summer came, we took Ranger and Danger, our three-inch painted turtles, with us to the creek, down to the place in the woods where the creek became a stream. We placed them on the muddy bank. Watched their red-striped necks stretch out in excitement and their little webbed feet begin to move and then, to our glee, they'd start to gather speed, their needle-sharp claws pulling their little helmeted bodies step by waddling step toward the water.

Of course, we were afraid they would get away. That was the fun of it. We'd have to build stick and leaf barricades downstream. Though it felt big to us, it was a small stream, so the engineering was manageable, though it involved a lot of wet shoes, which we'd hear about later. Released upstream, the turtles, transformed into masterful movers in the water, would swim toward us—the clever human engineers. We'd guide them with sticks—into this deep pool, away from that mound of sticks. We immersed ourselves, as they did, in the world of the clear-running stream. Summers in Maryland were hot and humid, but the creek mud was cool. The woods were quiet.

Our turtles turned out to be ideal companions. We never lost them. For me, though I did not know it then, this was an exercise in experiencing freedom within constraint, risk within boundaries.

When the family had to move, for reasons never properly explained, we were too young to understand our feelings of displacement and too nice to show anger at our parents for ruining our lives. We just took our turtles to the stream, without comment, one last time. We said goodbye and let them go. At least the turtles would be happy.

That freedom, that swimming in the wild, that independence with a safe home waiting is not far from what I'd hoped for in love and not previously been able to achieve in marriage. I wanted marriage to be a place where two people could be individual, creative selves within the bounds of fidelity and mutual care, nurtured and supported by mutual love. Was that so complicated? I found myself, my beloved and I found each other, made a life together on this place. So now the question remains: Who will we be if we have to leave?

Patterns of Recognition

One day last summer as I was walking by our meadow—which is what becomes here of unmowed grass—I saw a snaking channel moving in the long, waving grass. Some countercurrent moving underneath. Something, in some invisible level, was tunneling along, going to work or coming home, living his life right in front of me, completely out of sight. Mrs. Rocky? At the sound of my voice, the movement stopped. And sure enough, a fat raccoon rose up, bearlike, beady black eyes staring through her mask like a burglar surprised at a safe. I spoke again. She regarded me for another moment. Then, perhaps computing the familiar voice and form as the person who, in the evenings, up on the deck, hands her and her family pieces of bread, she casually lowered herself and went on her way through the almost-concealing grass.

Something about the encounter made me curious, and I retrieved an old sickle from the back shed and, just on an impulse, sliced into a section of grass. There, beneath the silky surface lay a network of well-traveled roadways. Little paths just wide enough for a cat-sized creature, a rabbit, or raccoon. They must follow their exact routes day after day, guided by their own scents, led by their own tracks, moving safely forward across the patterns of their past.

How like them am I? What inner pathways am I following daily, unknowing, unquestioning, while my surface mind is blinded by the turbulence of events? Is there, underneath my mind's habitual chaos, some labyrinth of pathways, some pattern that makes sense?

Lately, in the waking, semi-conscious gloom, I have no idea where I am. Or why. As if there's been a terrible mistake. As if some crazed bus driver zigzagging wildly through an unfamiliar city had dropped me in an unfamiliar neighborhood to fend for myself. As if I had been placed in a basket and left at the door of strangers. Who am I? What am I doing here?

Wild animals know themselves in their patterns. I have read of wolves, in the north, whose paws, over generations, have worn paths into solid rock. Who do they become when airdropped into some new territory? Do they venture forth, secure in their sense of direction or not, or do they stay, turning round and round in the circle of their own known tracks? I imagine them sniffing the trail, looking around for traces of kin. Shivering. I feel like that now, in the moment that bridges into daylight from the world of dreams. I want to run back, but the door to the dream is shut. I would like to, like the wolf, sit, raise my head to the stars, and howl.

But then the phone rings. Or someone walks into the room. Or I remember the date on the calendar and my appointment at nine. Daily life, with its problems and obligations, floods in and over the inchoate forms of the dark, and off I go, propelled as through a starting gate of some unidentified race. Am I "on track" or in some unconscious, automatic mode that leads to nowhere?

"We live our lives illogically forward and logically backward," a wise photographer friend once said. He was laughing at his own and all our bumbling efforts as we grope into the future, then how, with the brilliance of hindsight, we look back on what has turned out to be a perfectly plotted path. Or so it seems if we've followed our own, authentic inner guide.

Nature works this way. I know some blackbirds who lay their eggs season after season in a field that the farmer must plow right at the time the nestlings are starting to fledge. No amount of early waving or blowing of horns will convince the birds to alter their pattern and lay their eggs in the unfarmed field ten degrees or so to the north. They stay with the known, though it kills them.

I used to think they were stupid. Tiny little blackbird brains. What do they know? Now I read that that field was originally a wetland. Protected. The birds have for generations had the right to the place. They're grandfathered in. The farmer, in planting there, has, however unknowingly, overstepped his bounds. Some people are now making a case for the birds. As the birds, in their insistence, have helped me make the case for myself.

Illogical as my choices may seem on the surface, it may just be that underneath, down layer after layer under the easy understanding of things, certain indelible loves carve certain ineluctable paths. These paths lie—underneath everything, underneath the lostness, underneath the dead ends, underneath the sloughed off layers of a complicated life—unerring, drawing all the other layers of surfaces slowly, invisibly as the movement of tectonic plates, toward that one, uncompromisable, loved thing.

6

The First Offer

This morning, with the house having been "on the market" for almost two months, the real estate man has called us in to his office. He has an offer for us to review. "It's not what you're hoping for," he said, gesturing for us to sit down at his long pine contract-signing table, "but the buyer is qualified."

We were torn between panic and dread. Did this mean it will really be sold? So soon? We'll be relieved of our financial burden but left without a home? Or not? As the man fumbled for things in his desk drawer, I watched him, hoping for some clue about this offer. Was it good? Low ball? Close? But his face was inscrutable. Pensive and quick, on the thin side, with steady gray eyes, he had the look of someone who spent most of his time with numbers but longed to belong to a rock band. His graying hair hung just a bit longer than you would expect of someone in the business of selling properties—just touching the collar of his sports jacket—and his jeans were pressed. Though this was a dirty jeans and boots town, he wore hush puppies, and that gave him a sense of gliding about, making no waves. With his calmness intact, he placed the pages of a signed offer on the table and slid them over to me.

I glanced at the front page, took in the low number, felt my face blanch, and slid it over to my husband. We then looked at each other and then at our agent.

"Is this the best we can expect?" my husband asked, with a look that could have been interpreted as hostile unless one understood his normal British righteousness.

"It depends," said the real estate man, "on how badly you need to sell and how badly they want the house. It's like a dance."

Moment of silence.

My beloved and I again glanced at each other, and I said, pushing my chair back, my Washington D.C. assertiveness asserting itself, "We'll let you know."

The man nodded, blandly. "Okay. Take your time."

But as we rose, he added, "But not too much time. These things move fast."

Once outside, standing on the wooden sidewalk, my husband and I looked at each other. What to do? We may need to sell. But not at that price. Was the buyer crazy? My instinct told me that a better offer is sure to come along. But was I wrong? My husband, cautious in all matters, especially important ones, like American real estate, said, "Maybe we should call your father."

"Again?"

My father was a real estate man. I grew up listening to stories about houses. Buyers. Sellers. Deals. Dramas. For my father, real estate was a field of unending fascination about the value of property and the nature of the human being. When he came home, he could not stop himself from telling stories about his deals in minute detail over dinner till our eyes glazed over. The fascination of his transactions did not entirely define him but seemed to ignite his creative process. He saw the characters, he relived the acts—what he said, what she said, what they did next. Fork poised over her dinner plate, my elegant mother would yawn and say, "Oh, dear, let's ask what the girls did in school today." Thwarted, his face would darken, and he'd rise, take his dinner plate over to the kitchen counter to eat alone. Everyone hated this. There he'd be, standing over there, swaying back and forth in glowering silence, stabbing at his peas, and my sister and I would have to think up something worthy and entertaining that happened in history or math class. Truth is, we got more out of his stories than ours.

Like his story about the guy whose quirky old house he couldn't sell, couldn't sell, couldn't sell. Needed to sell but couldn't sell. Then, in came an interested buyer, and my father right away wrote up a contract. The buyer was eager. Made a good offer. But the owner wouldn't sign. Nope. Nope. He kept asking for more. He drove my father crazy. Daddy needed the deal. And the owner needed to sell but found something wrong with every revised offer submitted by the sole interested buyer. The more the obstinate owner resisted, the more the sole buyer just was determined to have the house. My father wrote up contract after contract, each time with some new, enticing provisions, and each time, the owner refused. Finally, one Friday night, when my father was alone in his office frowning over the stack of failed offers that burgeoned this owner's file, he heard a roar, just outside the office door. He got up and went to look. *Ho—ly cats* (his favorite expression) *Will ya look at that!* There, at the curb, sat the determined buyer astride a gleaming, growling 1936 twin-engine Harley Davidson Knucklehead. Daddy dropped his pen and ran outside.

The guy, leaning on the handlebars, said, "I'm about done. You're gonna write me up one last offer and then that's it."

Daddy went nuts. "Forget it," he said. "You're going to do just what I tell you, and by tonight, the house will be yours." (He pronounced it "yers.")

An hour later, at the quirky house with the lopsided porch and the windows askew, the unmistakable rumble of the Harley reached the owner's ears, and he jumped up from his dinner table and ran out the door.

"Well, wadda ya know," he cried. "Look at that!"

The frowning buyer sat astride his famous, vintage, manly machine, all muscle and shine, and the owner hurried over, walked around, studying every detail, whistling low, and then, squinting, said into the face of the rider, "Come 'ere." He gestured with his head toward the garage, which he'd kept locked and which held his collection—his *collection*, my father repeated, lifting his dark eyebrows up and down and smiling as he told the story—of Harley Davidson motorcycles. *Ooooh-ieee!*

My father sat outside in his Cadillac, humming and making little happy doodles on his yellow legal pad, while the buyer and seller, out in the garage, lost track of time, of the house, of the contract, of everything, bonding in their passion for Harley Davidsons.

And the deal? "Oh, sure," my father laughed. "The owner, happy as a clam, signed the original contract that night. No problems. *Haw haw.*" He laughed his head off. He just loved this. He loved the art of selling. Not because of the money. Alas for my mother, that almost didn't matter. He loved the dynamics. He loved the magic. He loved the mysterious something that makes someone want something enough to pay money—sometimes big money—to get it. Or not.

What, he often wondered, makes someone become willing to let go of something he has, for whatever reason, for whatever magically, exactly right, or grudgingly right price? What, one might wonder, is the magic that makes a genuine (pronounced gen-u-wine) salesman? Here's his best answer. It came, of course, in the form of another story. This time, we were all, my mother, my sister, and I, having lunch on a Saturday, after some outing, at Howard Johnson's, his favorite place.

The thing he loved about Howard Johnson's was that they were always the same. You knew just what's on the menu. "Here," he said, as we settled into our booth, "Get the waffles." He gestured for the waitress and then looked back at us. "Do you want to know how to tell a good salesman?" Our mother rolled her eyes. My sister and I nodded, resigned, knowing we would hear it anyway.

"So, I came in here yesterday," he said, leaning forward and giving each one of us a meaningful stare, "and I saw a man order a plate of pancakes." He waited a beat while a big smile spread across his face. "And wouldn't ya know, I'm looking over at the counter, and the waitress is putting down in front of this man—a big, fat man—this plate of pancakes. Three big ones, one on top of the other. And I'm watching, see?" My mother is frowning at the menu, but my sister and I are watching our father and can picture the fat man, and we're starting to smile.

"And so, this man, he's a biiiig, fat man, like that guy up there." Daddy points to a big fat man spilling over the stool at the end of the counter. "So, he grabs the syrup" he says, while making the motion with his hand, his eloquent, graceful hand, with the sapphire George Washington University law school ring—"pours the syrup on like this, and then..."—big eyes, big smile—"then he cuts the stack in four, like this," as he makes a cut vertically. "And like this," he makes a cut horizontally. Two neat swipes with the imaginary knife. "And then, he takes his fork and stabs one whole quarter stack..."—stab, stab—"and shovels the entire bite into his mouth." Big chomping motion. "Just like that." He waits for our laugh. "Then two bites more. Then, one last bite." He gazes at us to register our amazement. "Yep. In four bites, this big fat man has consumed an entire stack. Now that's what makes a great salesman."

We stared a little blankly at his conclusion. But my father could make a meaningful connection between two seemingly unrelated things with ease. And so, delighted with himself, he explained. "This man, I could see right there at the Howard Johnsons counter, has the drive to grab what he wants, to bite off huge challenges, to complete a task in a fraction of the time it would take normal people. Why, he can devour life." Big grin. And there, in one stack of pancakes—imagine the glow—was the secret of success.

My father did not consider himself a success. He did not devour life the way some people do until their desire sickens them. He did not wolf it down. He sniffed it. He hunted it, turned it over, and considered it. He stalked it like a cat. But he did not bite down hard. And so success, in the common understanding, kept escaping him. And yet, somehow, while he was never what you could call reliable, he never failed to offer just the right advice at just the right time.

When I first told him our troubles—the economy getting bad for tech startups, etc.—his advice was simple: "You've got a rare place there. You could sell while the market's good. But whatever you do, don't ever, ever be late on your mortgage, and don't ever, ever, ever get foreclosed."

His warning had ignited our decision to sell. We were scared. But at this price? Should we take the lowball offer and be done with it all? Or hold out. Which was riskier?

When we called my father, he was cagey. "Just remember one thing. Value is about desire: what you have that somebody else wants. And what you have is a nice place in a rare location. And they're not making any more like that. So, for your place—which is unique—not everyone will want it. But someone will. And will pay too much," he paused and chuckled, "just like you did!" *Ha ha ha.*

"Well, that wasn't much help," I said, miserably, when we hung up the phone.

"Remember the hole," my husband said, cheerily.

Right.

The Nouveau Poor

The advantage of having your home open to the snooping public is that it is always, at least once a week, clean and neat. The disadvantage, of course, is that you see how lovely the place is and how terrible it is that you need to sell it. Parents and closest friends take this opportunity to say, "Well, you shouldn't be out in the boondocks, anyway." Or "We never could figure out what you were doing in the middle of nowhere." Or, my favorite, "Well, maybe next time, find a house with closets." My least favorite, "Oh well, we all knew this California thing was just an experiment," is not much worse than the most painfully well-meaning one, "You'll be better off somewhere not so far away from everything." That last one had both a ring of truth and wild misunderstanding: What is this "everything" we're supposed to be so far from, when everything we want is right here?

Our other artist friends have similar dilemmas. Everyone is "starving." Everyone is "scared." One friend said yesterday that he gets "... thirty e-mails a day from people just trying, like us, to survive." Is it the times, the place, the "market" or just us? Sure, his little "startup" company has fizzled out, along with our savings. And I knew my shifting career paths would take time. But, frankly, other than the house thing, we don't feel "poor." Are we, I ask myself, poor?

As you creep closer to various edges, you get curious about those already over it. You develop a chill of recognition (think of St. Damien, discovering his first leper spot) on hearing yourself utter foreign sentences like: "I can't afford it." Or even, "How much is that?" You begin to see that when we talk about the poor, we must acknowledge two groups.

First, there is the True Poor, who identify with the term and who've been that way for a long time, such as some people around here who make their homes under tarps in the pine woods, whose attitude is more accepting than that of the new, nervous group, whose circumstances don't quite fit. This is the second group. The Nouveau Poor. Us.

Exiled from the cushions of affluence, yet foreign to the ways of the True Poor, we Nouveau Poor are lost. While we may dress like old poor (dusty shoes, faded jeans) and slouch about the dusty streets of our town like the rest, we are fatally distinguished from the True Poor by certain slips of the tongue, certain inappropriate word combinations such as pairing the word "need" with words like "massage" and "vacation" and "new hard drive." The old poor combine the word "need" correctly, with words like, "work" and "food." Mildly aware of a certain existential dissonance, we Nouveaux folk are earnest about acknowledging our reality, often using intensifiers such as "*really*" with the words "can't afford it," or "have no money," as we pull out our credit cards.

A typical symptom of our situation is that we lack patience. My literary agent and I had a falling out this week. After a long and tense conversation about a proposal we were crafting together, I said, with leaking irritation, "I just don't want to waste my time on this forever." One black eyebrow lifted, she looked into my eyes with predatory lethality. "I consider that an insult," she said. "Maybe you should work with someone else." Thus concluded the conversation and the partnership.

Reflecting on the bad exchange, I felt guilty. Then I remembered her commenting recently that she may have to sell her Picasso if the other deal she'd been working on didn't come through. Poor thing. A thick, gilded business plan rests on her mantle, atop green sage leaves, with a green votive candle burning, while the large, naked lady gazes out, dispassionately, from a frame on the wall. I will take her advice. Desperate people make bad business fellows.

However, they make great guests. This week, we prepared an elaborate feast with two artist friends who, burdened with healthcare debt, had just gone bankrupt. He's a filmmaker and she's a painter and both are, like us, imports from the denser, tenser East come here to the West to find ourselves, lose our inhibitions and in the process, our fortunes. The filmmaker would now really like to be a massage therapist. The painter thinks chopping carrots in a restaurant would give her inner peace.

Neither she nor her husband has the required surface banter or glamorous looks, so becoming movie stars or car salesmen (a choice John Updike once commented upon, in relation to himself)—was not an option, except maybe to Robert. So, there we were, all doing what we set out to do, and the results, good and bad, are unfolding according to our fates.

The Origins of Squalor

We had another offer last week. It seemed good, dollar-wise, but the buyers' finances seem a bit dodgy, and they wanted concessions. We consulted the Real Estate Man and our higher selves, and decided, in for a penny, in for a pound, we'd hold our line. Again, the Real Estate Man suggested we might put some more effort into spiffing up the place—an effort I truly detest—beautifying my home so someone I don't know and don't want to know can come in, traipse about, judging, critiquing, tapping their pencils on their teeth, comparing.

If I could conduct my own "house tour," it would go like this.

Welcome to my lovely, expensive, West Marin home, I'd say, with a toothy smile. *What do you mean, "Don't I have a lawnmower?" That's not a ratty, unkempt lawn! That's a meadow! It was beautiful this spring, you should have seen it. I had hundreds of different kinds of grasses and wildflowers. Each week offered a new surprise as various species appeared, matured, and strangled others. The meadow was waist high at last year's peak. Deer moved through and you'd only see their ears. You probably don't have that in San Francisco. Or wherever you're escaping from.*

But come on up. You'll love the deck. Just step over the apple cores and around the blue corn chips, and don't mind the messy stains around the dish, which is named "Pussy" but is really for Rocky, the raccoon, and her four babies, Foxie and her three, and, when he comes around, Old Yellow Cat.

On a busy evening, the raccoon family will be on the top deck, scooping out the dish, taking the bread from my hands in their delicate fingers, while the fox will be trotting back and forth in the lower shadows. Old Yellow Cat, when he's not out killing something, will be watching from the bougainvillea planter frowning. I know, I know, rabies, dirty deck, all that, still, however illicit, this social contact with the wild is bracing.

But hey, don't be shy! Come in, come in, welcome to our beautiful California home. Vast open space, is it not? Cathedral ceilings, lots of glass, kitchen over there, dining room table here, living room just beyond that little round table. Yes, there is a table there. It's under that pile of books, magazines, letters, notices, an underwater camera, a plate, some plastic bags, files, glasses, notebooks, old Atlantic Magazines, New Yorkers, sections from the New York Times, a current, half-eaten sandwich, and a TV guide. This pile exists so that the dining room table—six feet away—can remain pristine. You could look at this pile, mound, really, as a visual representation of the shadow side of neatness. The wise do not scorn it but learn to accept it. In times of denial, we focus on the dining room table in its Zen-like emptiness. In times of self-loathing, we focus on the mound. Both are false, both are true. But come, let me show you around.

I'd like to offer you something to eat, but I've just noticed, as I open the refrigerator door, that everything in there is dead. Withered lettuce stuck to the rungs, a scraggly fistful of carrots, a jar of jam, some plastic bags of liquefied vegetation, soy milk in a caved in looking cardboard box, and a couple of covered mystery pots, with the dreaded Who-Knows-What inside. In the good old days, in civilized Washington, Gladys, my housekeeper, would have taken care of this. Now, I am so upset at the amount of stuff to do that I do not wish to address the refrigerator at all. I just open it up, grab something, and shut the door quickly, so I do not see what may be moving, lurking, reproducing there, in the dark, like a hideous enemy.

Oh. Don't look in that corner, where the newspapers, the Wellingtons, the toolbox, the orange power cord, the water bottles and the actual brooms and mops are all spilling out of the unfinished closet. That will someday be shelves where the kitchen appliances will reside. Things like the electric juicer (which I used for a month) the blender (which I never use now that I know I am allergic to bananas) and the coffee grinder (buying the local roast already ground saves time). These are good looking, useful things that will make this kitchen seem like a place where someone cooks. But for now, to tell you the truth, I don't notice this corner anymore, eyesore that it is. I blot it out. I just toss the newspapers down onto the pile with deliberate disrespect. Because I know, when I stare at the grungy amalgam, that the planned shelves lie far, far in the future.

That future is extended by the lengths of time it will take my fine artist, brilliant intellectual and supremely organized Pisces husband to find or create proper storage spaces for each and every single item piled therein. Living with a Pisces distorts one's sense of time.

Let me explain. Do you see that woodpile out there? Not the pile of neatly cut firewood which remains where it was dumped at the edge of the property, but the pile right here, all those greyed boards that cover most of the yard. No, I don't mean what's under the blue tarpaulin (which is long enough to house an Airstream trailer). That's trash. That's waiting to be taken to the dump. It's been waiting for six months now, so perhaps it is ready. Ha ha. We cannot take the trash to dump until The Pisces has gotten his Company funded. I know. Don't question this. We're talking about the boards. There is no point moving them until they are all categorized, and we know where each type will go and have created a specific place for each. And that, I am informed, will take thinking through. "It's a piece of work," for a Pisces. I, myself, wanton Gemini that I am, would—and may still—stack them all up under the house and go inside and read a book. Fire hazard be damned! Someday later, when we need a board, I'd go have a look at what we've got. Meanwhile, every time I open the back door, my field of vision is filled with reminders of work unfinished, rubble uncleared, tasks un-faced and healthy physical labor shunned. And I say to myself: I am living in squalor.

Do I sound like a harping wife? Yes! Am I moving the boards? No! Am I living in squalor? Well . . .

The Monkey Trap

The Buddhists talk about how easy it is to catch a monkey. First, you learn his weakness: sweets, delicacies of any kind, honey, crumpets, you name it. Second, you understand how fierce the monkey is in his determination to have what he wants. Once he gets his goodie in his grasp, he will never let it go.

That's all you need to know. Then you make a little cage. Or it could be a jar. Inside, you place the wonderful, sweet thing, the thing he knows he cannot live without, the thing he craves above all, the thing he must have. Set it nicely inside. If it is a cage, close the door. The bars are just far enough apart so that the delicate little monkey hand can reach right in. Same with the opening of the jar. Just wide enough for that spidery little hand to reach in and circle around the sweet. Ah.

What happens next could make you laugh. Watch closely: There is the cage, with its secret little sweet; there is the clever monkey, reaching so eagerly inside; then there is a terrible commotion. You rush up and say, "Ah ha! You thieving monkey, I've caught you at last! I'm going to grab you and kill you and cook you for dinner!" And the monkey has two thoughts: 1) to be grabbed and killed and cooked sounds terrible indeed, but 2) he must not lose hold of his treat. So he grips it in his fist and holds on.

Problem. The fist doesn't fit through the opening.

The monkey struggles ferociously to free the fist that holds the sweet, but the space between the bars is only wide enough to admit his open hand. "Let it go," part of you urges him, "and you will be free!" The monkey, although smart enough to see this, is blinded by his appetite. "Too bad," you say, "but the choice was yours." Then you kill him and eat him for dinner.

Buddhists are so wise.

Once I went sailing with a man who said he knew boats. I was a little afraid because I could barely swim, but he said not to worry, he knew boats. He rented the sloop at a pier on the Severn River, settled me in, piled bag lunches and a cooler in the hold and cast off. A wind came up. My throat slammed shut. The man who knew boats yelled, "Hold on tight!" Defying the wind, he pulled on the mainsheet with all his weight. The wind pushed at the sail and the boat heeled way over. I clung to the gunwales in dread. As the "captain" pulled tighter and tighter, the angle of mast to water became more and more acute until finally, the boat flopped over flat, as if the sail had been arm-wrestling with the wind.

As brown bay waters closed over my face, my emergency nervous system began flashing red: Shipwreck! Drowning. Lost At Sea. Death! When I surfaced, gasping, my eyes, in and out of the brackish waves were level with a gaily bobbing line of little donuts, a flotilla of plain, chocolate-covered, powdery-white and honey-dipped donuts, all liberated from the hold of the sailboat where our stashed brown lunch bags, suddenly liberated, spilled their contents into the choppy waters, sending them merrily, merrily downstream.

In the bubbling midst of what surely would be my last gasp, the sight of the bobbing donuts made me laugh. And laughing drove the panic from my throat and slowed the thrashing of my limbs, and I found myself swimming, pleasantly, almost pleasurably, among the floating contents of the shipwreck. Thanks to a passing fishing boat and amidst many guffaws at the stupid "captain," we were eventually towed to shore, seaweed dripping from the mast.

I take in these lessons this morning. I wouldn't be stupid as a monkey, would I? "Don't hold on!" Of course not. I'm not stubborn as that arrogant phony sailor, am I? Hell no! I would not hold fast, straining harder and harder in the same direction while waters of circumstance threaten to drown me. Would I?

The Known and the Unknown

For some time now, I have coexisted peacefully with a spider on my windowsill. I have been respectful of his web and that of his neighbor beside him, but today that relationship has become more complex.

As I emerged from the house, the sky was in rapture. All across my view, fog and sun were lying upon each other like lovers, breathing, rolling, glowing, showering luminance over everything. The path to my Casita was draped with glistening "spiders' doilies"—little webs draped in the bushes—and long, glistening spiders' lines that I walked through with apologies to the spinners whose work I must so crudely undo. Even the blackberry brambles glistened in the shafts of sun. What a night the spiders have had! The little round apple tree was entirely draped with their filaments of light. High at the tip of one of its branches, a perfect, shining web, the size of an out-stretched hand, was hanging, and waved at me, as if hailing a taxi.

Pausing in the mist to study the webs and marvel at the spiders' mastery of design, I was about to resist comparing their genius to that of humans and then remembered something truly odd I'd recently read. A NASA team of scientists had—believe it or not—recently performed experiments where groups of spiders were fed, respectively, Benzedrine, caffeine, and marijuana. The results of the drugs on their brains showed plainly in their webs. Those on speed wove their webs with great gusto but left big holes. Those on pot started out well enough but seem to have lost interest halfway through. Those on caffeine, however, seemed to have staggered around, incapable of weaving anything but a few random strands that hung together more by accident than by design. The study, modeled after an earlier, 1948 experiment, pursued the question of whether the results of the arachnids' performance on mind-altering drugs might parallel that of human behavior.

These results, as with many science projects, arouse interest but raise more questions than they answer, such as: how do you serve coffee to a spider? And for me, looking down at my coffee cup steaming up at me with its great and promising aroma, do I dare take another sip?

I was thinking about spiders as I entered the Casita this morning and noticed a subtle change in the room. Over on the windowsill where the two spiders have been quietly inhabiting two identical funnel webs, only one seemed occupied—the spider, bug-eyed, peering out of his funnel, waving his little feet, the way children wave their feet out of car windows.

The other web seemed collapsed and looked oddly seedy. I looked in. Nobody home. So I took a dust rag and brushed the empty web away, leaving his neighbor's web safely intact.

To be clear: I am not a spider lover. Though at the Zen Center I chant with the others the Buddhist vow to "save all creatures," I am not someone who would decline to swat a mosquito that's landed on my arm. However, thinking as I do, almost all the time, about the meaning of home, I am not highly motivated to roust another creature, even a spider, from his. Also, when you look at a living creature every day, even as foreign a fellow as a spider, you start to wonder about him. You watch his habits. You root for him, as when a bee stumbles against the glass and is slightly snagged in the gossamer net, and the spider, a fourth his size, rushes him again and again, unsuccessfully. You admire his persistence. You can't dispatch a creature you've grown to know.

Still.

There is the matter of the unknown spider. Who could be anyone. Even someone very dangerous. I would not want to share my space with, say, a black widow spider, who can kill you, or make you wish you were dead. Or even worse, a brown recluse, whose bite causes necrosis in the flesh. What else might there be, lurking about in my space, the identity of which I did not know? Was I safe? With one spider missing from his web, on the loose, as it were, I decided to check out my spider friend in my full-color, illustrated *Field Guide to North American Insects and Spiders* to see what I could find out about him.

There are some very terrible spiders in this book: The rabid wolf spider, who looks like his name, is one you would not want to meet. Nor would you like to come face to face with the bola spider, with staring toady eyes, or the daring jumping spider, a musclebound hairy, eight-legged, gorilla-looking thing who can spring at you at any time. What if one of those is living in here now? Or the desert tarantula? Two inches of furry hideousness, crouching in a corner, watching me day and night. Would I amiably dust around *him*?

Actually, a tarantula, yes. On my karmic ledger, I owe one tarantula its life. It happened in Tortola. I was among six vacationing friends, and we were sleeping soundly—as one does in a Caribbean villa with all the windows open and the balmy air and ocean rhythms lulling you back to the womb—when a scream rang out. It came from the bedroom of Cyril, the psychoanalyst among us, known for spending most of his beach-combing days talking about his anxiety and collecting bones.

Doors banged open and the rest of us, struggling into our robes, ran through the halls toward the sound. Cyril's room was blaring with light, the bed turned upside down, and he and his wife, Joanie, were ripping off sheets, their faces drained. Panic, desperation, sheer terror electrified the air. "I've been bitten!" he hissed, clutching the side of his neck with his flattened palm. His pale eyes were wild, even more worried than usual. We pried away his hand and underneath, on the side of his neck, there were indeed two little red holes about an inch apart. Our skin crawled, and we glanced at the open window for signs of the escaping vampire. Aloud, we tried to reassure our friend with reasonable theories. None were pleasant. Bats could be rabid. Spiders kill. Beetles, well, they would just make one hole. What else?

No one slept for the rest of the night, and sometime after sun-up, after coffee and papaya, after Cyril and Joanie's room had been totally searched, after all the amateur medical and entomological theories had been exhausted, and the two little wounds had not swollen, nor had our friend shown symptoms other than his now livid anxiety, someone spied, in a corner, over the wooden molding of the door, brown as the Caribbean mahogany, furry as a Yeti, and the size of an open hand, a *tarantula*.

The six of us stared at him in a combination of horror, artistic fascination, and awareness of an ethical dilemma. First, none of us had ever seen a live tarantula before, and he was impressive. At least six inches across. Then, though the width of him and the space between what we assumed would be his fangs seemed to fit the size of the bite marks, how could we be sure this particular tarantula was the biter? Also, even if he was, what could we do? The thing crouching over the door was a creature of substance, too big, too furry, too personal to swat.

Still, if we were to stay in the house, the tarantula had to go. The only question was how.

I rummaged around outside and found a pool net. David, our ship's captain, grabbed the handle and aimed the net up toward the tarantula. We gathered around, craning our necks. High above our heads, he cringed as the net came toward him. Someone said, "Lookout! He's going to jump!" We all shrunk back. David thrust the handle of the net over at Allan, his pal, saying, in a manly voice, "Here, Allan, you do it." Allan looked around, swallowed, and took it. "OK, everyone. Don't move!" We called advice from afar. "Ease him out nicely," someone said. After all, none of us wanted him biting our necks. "Let him know we mean well," someone else said, fearing spiders' revenge. The person who went for the book stood in another doorway and called out, "It says tarantulas eat about a hundred pounds of bugs a day." But are they poisonous? No!

"His bite is like a bee sting." Still . . .

"Gently!"

"Don't hurt him,"

"For God's sakes, don't squish him against the wall."

Then, suddenly, the creature braced itself to leap.

Everybody screamed.

Our leader slammed the pool net over the tarantula, who tumbled into the pool net and thrashed around a bit as a person might hitting a fireman's net after a twenty-story fall. Allan carefully, carefully closed the net over itself, trapping the tarantula inside and then lowered the net to the floor. We all clustered around for a look.

A close, careful examination of any animal cannot help but reveal its beauty. Even a tarantula. Eight shining, furry legs, eyes that made up a kind of face. Beautiful. Entomological perfection.

But what to do? Six converted tarantula-lovers paraded out the front door of the villa and down the long white cement walk following a bouncing pool net, with the tarantula clinging to the side. Where to put him?

"Here's a spot!"

"No, too sunny."

"Here's a spot!"

"No, too shady."

Suddenly, Allan, the tarantula-bearer, tripped, the pool net fell, the happy tarantula sailed out in a blissful arc, landing in the middle of the bright white walkway where he sat, stunned, free, and blinking in the blinding sun. Almost immediately, from out of nowhere, cleaning buckets and mops clanging at her sides, flapped a large native lady wearing flip-flops.

The six of us froze as she approached. Far away inside the house, Bob Marley was lilting cheerfully, "We'll be to-ge-thah...da-de-DA-DA-da-de-de-de-dah..." Down the walk she came, flap, flap, flap. Spying the known tarantula, our tarantula, the native lady sang out, "Wass dees?" and without skipping a beat, lowered her fat, black flipper down and squashed him underfoot.

What is to be learned from this? Are humans doomed to be forever, as someone once said of Woody Allen, "At two with nature?"

But of course, the spider in my studio is not a tarantula. He is a funnel builder, the book says. The black widow and the brown recluse and my spider all are "funnel builders" too. They build the kind of webs you often see outdoors, a big Halloweeny kind of web with a neat funnel in the middle where the spider hides. There are hundreds of funnel builders. If you believe the book, their behaviors differ. Some are aggressive, some are shy. Mine, I think, are shy. But so are brown recluses. You can tell them apart by size and color, and this is not easy. Colors vary. The black widow male has some white stripes, and of course the female has the red hourglass—but the immatures are brown with white stripes. The brown recluse is really kind of yellow. I can never discern the "violin" they talk about. My spider, I decided, having none of those distinguishing marks, is (I hope) a grass spider, the kind that usually lives out-of-doors and is (I think) harmless.

So why, you might ask, all this about spiders? Perhaps the tension of late is loosening my screws, but I like it when I come into my little studio early in the morning and I can see two little spiders peeking out from their funnels on my windowsill, waving their feet. Their foreignness is such that they have no similar awareness of me, unlike the birds and deer and raccoons and everything else around, not to mention the man up in the house who will be upset if I don't join him for breakfast. The spider, safe in his web, an entity in a universe of his own, asks nothing but to be let alone, to get on with his waiting, and as such, is a pleasing sight.

Alas, there is more to this tale. There is also the spider over there on the wall!

Is it "my" spider? Or some unknown spider? With a shock, I realize that my laissez faire "relationship" with the spider in the web on the windowsill, if indeed the fellow on the wall is the same spider, just gone from his web, has now changed. He is not in his place, where I can see him, predict his movements, where he is "my spider." He is now the unknown spider, out there, somewhere abroad in the room, where he can watch me. Can scare me. I know that if he should show up on my laptop keyboard, or if I should lift some papers and find him there, I may—however involuntarily and despite my inter-species magnanimity—swat him dead.

Crossing from "known" to "unknown," the spider loses his "civil rights." I regret this but can't help it. And I can't help thinking, in the larger, human realm, of the consequences, conscious and unconscious, of moving from the known to the unknown, from home, where one is named and known, to the outside, where no one is known, and everyone is a stranger. Again, the whispered question: *When we leave here, who will we be?*

The Importance of Names

Morning sun. Warm winds. Crows mobbing an owl somewhere off in the pine tops. The mesa is waking. Blue-eyed grass (which is blue with yellow middles) and golden-eyed grass (which is yellow with yellow middles) wink up through green grass spears. I try not to step on them with my heavy lobsterman's boots on the way to the cliff.

This spring, instead of saying, *Oh, the yellow things are blooming*, I have decided to find out their names. I realize this is like discovering a new best friend at a goodbye party, but still, I go to the cliff this morning with my flower book. Grass is thick now and ankle high. I meet a small, four-petaled yellow blossom, low to the ground, sunk in the dew, with fat leaves. I look it up.

There are several pleasures in identifying a flower. First, you go through page after page of beautiful color illustrations of exotic blossoms, which is pleasant. Then, as you do, you notice the little plant at your feet, waiting, open-faced, for you to discover its name. I think of dogs or children, smiling, looking up expectantly for a word of praise. Aware of this, I proceed very carefully through the pages, alternating scrutiny of the photographs with examination of the flower itself. Studying a flower is like studying the face of someone sleeping. You watch very quietly until its own personal charm reveals itself to you. This is what you wait for, much as you, yourself, wait for someone to discover and praise your own particular charm.

This little yellow flower with its four neat, golden petals, is called a "sun-cup." Sun-cup, I say to myself as I pass one after another in the field. Sun-cup. You might carelessly trample a weed, but you would never step on a sun-cup. The field begins to be enlivened by a multitude of sun-cups, whom I now know by name.

Another little yellow flower baffles me. Nine oblong petals, a little crowned center, spindly leaves. Nothing like it in the book. I try to find it as it waits, but finally, move on, concerned. I do not want to leave a flower unnamed. Suddenly, here's another. Ah. Same flower, but with compound leaves. Perhaps the one I've just seen has simply started shedding petals. This, the book reveals, is a California buttercup. So very different from the ones I knew growing up in metropolitan Washington, the kind you hold under your chin to see if you "like butter."

Scattered through the grasses are clouds of small flowers with silvery, multi-fingered leaves that look like miniature lupines. Then I come upon one with a pale lavender and white cone-shaped blossom made up of pea-shaped flowers. It's a lupine, but a far cry from the splendid purple spires that covered the fields in the summers in Maine. Hardship—the continual western wind, the pounding sun, the droughts—seems to have forced this plant back to minimal stature. Still, the similarity is exciting. Plant life, as well as memory, spans the continent.

Down in a glen, so elegant and delicate as to be out of place in this rough field, are luscious clumps of wild purple (Douglas) irises.

Irises. Now here is a bit of science. First, this delicate peninsula in which my home is nestled, is a place of microclimates. Our friends, for example, a half mile over on the southeast edge of the mesa, facing the reef, live in a roar of constant winds, fog, mist, and chill. Imagine Cornwall in a gale. They can grow nothing but the toughest vines, cypresses, and coastal pines, things that like to hang on and wrestle with the wind. But our neighbor, the same distance over to the west, whose land is a long, south-facing slope, grows grapes. You go there and stand in the blue rows of lavender and think you are in Provence. Where we live is more like Wiltshire in the summer. Protected, but chill, sunny but not balmy, willing, but reserved. Rosemary thrives here. And all the Australian bushes like my tea tree bushes and the grand eucalyptus.

And irises.

The odor of an iris is unnerving. It opens a chute in my memory and sends me down, down, far back into a quiet garden in the outskirts of D.C. proper, in a place that is now a bank. There was a walnut tree at one corner in the back garden, a row of rose bushes, taller than I was, in the front, and along the side, a rock garden with hens-and-chickens and irises.

"Flag lilies," he called them, the gentle man in slippers and striped pajamas and the dark-blue terry cloth robe. Granddaddy was delicate, perennially convalescent, either recovering from his last operation or getting ready for the next. He was finicky, wanting often only a half a boiled egg. He was vigilant: "Is that a draft? I feel a draft." He wanted us children all bundled up, lest we "catch our death of cold."

He spent his days in his chair, books of science opened on his lap, lost in his thoughts as the women chattered about the house. The garden was his escape. The iris was his flag. I was his companion in seeing. A veteran of World War I, who ran a field hospital during its last days in France, was recovering, I think now, from life.

A picture of him, at fifteen, in a wide hat and jodhpurs, sitting outside a tent somewhere in Panama in the Spanish-American war, shows a boy's face that looked, even then, as though his stomach hurt. He was not musical, so perhaps his Irish melancholia had to play upon his physique. The same tense face, now Captain Burke, in full dress uniform, stared at us children through an oval frame hung by the front door, even as Granddaddy dozed opposite in his chair. Did he dream of battles and gunfire and horses falling under him screaming? Did he see his mother, desperate for a new world, herding her children into the steerage of a ship that would carry them from Galway to New York?

Did he dream of some new world too? Did he think, after all of it, that after what he'd seen, the world had gotten better? His taciturn attitude would indicate not. "Put 'm to work," he'd say, walking past a radio over which Frank Sinatra crooned.

As a person always on call for death, he had no time for fools. But when he could walk and the weather was mild, he had time for his garden, for the flag lilies and me, his first grandchild.

Aware of the privilege of his attention, I said very little around him, but I watched him and listened, loving the musical sound of his voice. He held my hand and led me around the garden, and we looked at each blossom a long time, examining the furry tongues, noting the differences of color, the incredible drooping petals, the strange scent. He taught me their names. Each one had a face. Things with faces are persons.

I felt the flag lilies look back.

When they played Taps, and his spirit flew away with those terrible notes over the hills of Arlington Cemetery, I didn't know what to do. I felt left behind as on another planet, among weeping people who forgot I was even there. People think children don't grieve. That's not true. They just don't know how. So they stay quiet or act out, and people think they're odd.

I planted irises all over this place in honor of my grandfather. I think of him now as I count my days here, and I see him in his garden with his irises and his little granddaughter, counting his days, the days of his earthly life. As we stop at each flower, I see him transferring parts of his spirit into me as if he could lift his hat and draw from his head invisible handfuls of vision and place them into mine.

Mysteries of Time and Space

Last night, I lay awake, as is often the case now, looking through the wide expanse of windows to where the clear night was sprinkled with stars. Stillness. Vastness. Presence. Presence of what?

Once, in my previous life as a producer of films and media back in the East, I had occasion to interview a famous physicist about time and space. As we were setting up lights for the camera, I asked him my "dumb blonde" question: What's in space? I was genuinely curious about what—in the vast emptiness between the stars and planets and asteroids and general stuff up there—what is in Space? To my surprise, instead of laughing, as I thought he would, his eyes lit up and he paused and then, looking around as if scanning a room for a lost pair of glasses, started saying a number of scientific-sounding things that boiled down to, as he summed it up: *Intelligence.*

As I recall the moment—and because the exchange occurred before we rolled tape so I have no transcript to confirm—he said the word with such fullness that any question, any poking at the word for further definition, further juice, would have been rude, if not useless.

The word was enough. It confirmed what I have always felt when I look up at the stars, or I listen to the silence. That the silence is full of something. The emptiness is full of something.

7

Seeing in the Dark

I once knew a photographer—legally blind—who took pictures in order to see. On almost any given day, in the outer room of a bustling communal lab, you would find him crouched in a corner with a newly made black-and-white print clasped up against his face. He would be scrutinizing it like a jeweler through a loupe held tight to his one barely functioning eye. He would travel the loupe over the picture inch by inch, letting his mind piece together an image out of the gray-black blur that was his world. In this way, he assembled for himself images of children in parks, women on sofas, mothers in kitchens, and us, his friends.

Each picture he took tickled him. "So, this is Dawn!" he'd cry, squinting through his loupe over what might be an earring or a part of a sleeve. "Hey, here's David!" And his loupe would have just moved from the beard to the hand holding the glass of rum. He had a way of recognizing, in details, the essence of the whole.

Sometimes, even for those with perfect vision, the world is unclear until put in a frame. We don't know what we see until we have seen it. The photograph in front of me now, for example, I study the way the blind man did: to see what the camera has seen that my eyes could not.

It is only a snapshot, one of those color glossies taken with the automatic camera that someone handed me in the room when I suddenly looked around, helpless, having neglected to bring my own. The little borrowed camera had a zoom lens, so I could stand a polite distance from my subjects, while bringing the image in tight so that the two faces could fill the vertical frame. At first glance, you might see them as Madonna and child, the Madonna's dark hair outlined against a stark background, the child's hairless white head pressed against the Madonna's dark cheek. A pieta. Only here, the roles were reversed.

The young Madonna's mahogany eyes confront the lens with the kind of look you see in photographs of women huddled in war or famine. I look into these eyes now, in the photograph, as I could not then, in that room, even though the eyes are the eyes of my friend. I look at her from behind the mutual safety of the camera and imagine down her ancestral lines, a Magyar tribesman dashing through mountain gorges on horseback, veils waving, sabers drawn. In the picture, only the slight lift of the finely arched brows hints at a possibility of helplessness, giving her warrior's eyes a shocked, resigned, perhaps pleading look, as of someone about to be run through.

She clutches the other figure to her the way a child would clutch a doll or a hostage-taker a victim—as a shield. In this gesture, even if I did not already know it, I would recognize the Madonna as the daughter. And even if I did not know, I would see, in the ghostly similarity in their features, that the one she is holding is the one who gave her life.

Her mother's head looks large and hairless as a Buddha's. Drawn on it, like a cartoon drawn on a balloon, the same delicate brow, the same high bone just beneath the eye, the nose that could have been traced from the same Roman coin. But the pitch of the head suggests dead weight, and the eyes aim downward like marbles in a tilted bowl, as if directed no longer by the habit of interest, but by gravity itself. Not even the mouth, with its shining trail of drool, has the muscle to remain polite.

Anyone scrutinizing this photograph, as I am, might imagine, from the look of the two of them, that my friend has pulled her mother from a fire or a wreck of some kind that has left her stunned and scorched. Then you see the indentation that arcs across the skull like a sunken headband. This is where they sawed through and pried away the skull, removing it like a pot lid to reveal the tumor, a fat lotus, blossoming inside.

Here you stop a moment and wonder.

What happens when they remove the lid to someone's brain? Do images of their past just flutter out into the ether, like pages escaping from a book in wind?

Do lines of Hungarian poetry that she memorized in childhood simply waft into thin air? Are there pictures of Christmas trees with actual candles or the thudding of invading Russian soldiers stomping past the basement windows?

Or did she hold the sight of writhing babies covered in slime and blood? Or was there a special place in her brain for chamomile blossoms in sunlight on an Austrian hillside after the War? Do smells escape too, like the ones stashed there since childhood? Cake batter. Puppies' breath. Spit-up. The smell of sun on skin. Goulash.

This being her skull, might the notes of an aria from Puccini suddenly fill the operating room and go wafting through the atmosphere, looking for someone else who could use a good tune?

And when they clamped the skull back, letting the tumor get back to its dark meal, what happens if the memories get folded wrong, like pieces of crumpled paper, and can't be read again?

What do you have left? The terrible blank light of the hospital corridor? A longing for paprikas with hot dogs?

It seems crazy that a mass of matter not even out of nowhere, but part, let's not forget, of a life's own stuff, can chew, bite by bite, every last connection between that life and the outer world. Can sever all the chords that mediate between will and action, everything except, perhaps, that which causes a frown.

Denial, my friend used to say—back when her mother was healthy and she, herself, had the leisure to be angry with her—was her mother's problem. One of those things she should change. Get real. Denial, that balm, that ever-ready salve for the abrasions of daily life. Could the tumor be some ghastly extension of that wish to eradicate the unpleasant? Some out-of-control hitman who erases even the expression on the face? And without expression, can we know if there's anything left? Like the blind photographer, I need to look hard to see who this is I have photographed.

My friend and I talked later that August day, on her porch in humid Washington, D.C., over glasses of wine. "I don't know if she hears me," she said. I said, out of hope, more than knowing, "Her soul hears you." She nodded. We both believe this, want to believe this, but it does not help. She said, "I wish it were over."

Looking at the photograph, I do not believe her. I believe she wishes it never to be over.

I remember one night, some days before I took the picture, I visited her mother alone. She opened her eyes and stared at me. Hooked her gaze into me. Stark, impolite, the way the blind photographer used to stare at us, unseeing, yearning, like someone screaming behind the shut window of a fast-receding train. What? I wanted to say. What . . . ?

But she just stared.

And so my friend holds her unseeing mother on that terrible threshold, clinging to her against that inner push that would see the mother born, not into life, but out of it.

I didn't think any of this, taking the picture. I just considered the light, the distance. Watched for the right composition. Said, "Yes, that's right. That's good." Took the picture.

Only now, like the blind man, bent over the little print, do I begin to know how to say goodbye.

Living in Goodbye

I once knew a woman who was known for her beauty. She had that savage, black-haired, blue-eyed Irish face that could freeze men to silence or cause women to follow her anywhere. She was a teacher, a fine art photographer, known for her compositions of light and longing. White on white. Open windows with billowing curtains. Silken-haired children, turning away, clutching curtains or lace. She posed naked for her students, twirling in parachute silk. We were friends. Both photographers, but our work was different. I photographed portraits with a big camera, straight. I liked to find just the right spot in the landscape, just the right quality of light, of form, and put the subject there and wait, in the anonymity of the dark cloth, for the moment when the person in front of me exhaled, blinked, allowed the lens to see.

Once, when I was making such a portrait of her, she shocked me into tears. The scene was an empty house—her venue of choice. As I was behind the cloth, focusing, she said, out of the blue, "Every time I take a photograph, I'm saying goodbye."

Stunned, I looked out from behind the camera, tears rolling uncontrollably down my face.

She said, surprised, "You?"

Me? Cry? I was the one who always made her laugh. But her words, the moment, collapsed me. I couldn't say why. I just laughed and shrugged. "We're done," I said, and put the camera away. Perhaps the moment revealed something about her I must have known and did not want to see. We never spoke of it again. But when she died a few months later, in a car crash, late at night, a half mile from her home, her words resounded in my mind.

I'd like to talk to her about that moment now. Those words. What she really meant. So different from what I think (if I think) when I bring my camera up to my eye. When I see a moment of light or a gesture in a person I'm watching, the "click" for me is not about "goodbye," but rather something more like—*stay*. Everything is passing. Even this "I" I think myself to be is just passing through—a thought that, while I know it is true, somehow, I can't believe. So I deceive myself and beg everything to conspire with me to *stay*.

When I lift the camera, I want that moment to stay. When I am in my darkroom and the image comes up as I rock the chemicals in the red light, I say, *there you are!* The live person may be on a plane to Australia, but in my developer, *there he is*. The photograph, hanging up to dry or in a frame, looking back at me.

There we are, in that moment, and *here we are*, you, in the frame, and I... I in my frame of time, holding this dripping image of you. You, the subject, who are in another plane of time, or timelessness. Something of your essence, or the essence that occurred in our earthly exchange, remains, and I feel you there, in the image, looking back at me. You are there. I was there. And in the print, the moment is fixed. Time stopped.

People hold time in different ways. A painter I knew wanted to possess the moment, take it away with him, make something new. I photographed him once, making one of his grand large-scale paintings, from beginning to end. He had as his subject matter a large swath of the north woods, with lakes and rivers, rocks and trees and clear Maine blue sky above. He made huge canvasses, eight feet by eight, or even larger.

He took me out in the woods with him one day, so I could photograph him making the first sketch. On a small, twenty-four-by-twenty-four-inch canvas propped up on his easel, he made a comprehensive study with a thin brush, capturing the essence of what that spot was about—the lines, the forms, the angle of the light, where the rock was, how covered with moss was it, whether it was in light or shadow, was there a mushroom, and was there blue sky, were there puffy white clouds, how white, where were the shadows, were the leaves turning red, how red, and were the trunks of the birch trees gray or white, what colors were in the gray in the shadows of the rock?

All that, he got. But that was just a study, not the painting itself, which he made in his huge barn studio. The painting was not only about the woods but about the fact of painting the woods. And about woods. And about time. And about the history of art. But mostly, to me, as an observer, it was about a moment in place, about holding on to that place and time. But that's not how he saw it. He said once, "When this painting is finished, that place is over. It is finished for me."

For this painter, there was no "capturing of the moment." But there had been that "being in the moment" of that place, capturing the essence of that place on his canvas. All the way through the rest of his stages he seemed to have been digesting that moment and then making of it something new, something true to the moment, the place, but also to the relationships of the forms and colors on the canvas and of his place in the world of art and... of himself. I look at the finished painting and I feel the painting. I feel the woods. The light. And though I could be projecting, in the care of each brush stroke applied with absolute consciousness, I feel his love of the woods. Of the paint. The smell of it. The silky feeling of the brush as he lays it on and moves the color in. And while the moment may be long past, the presence—I feel—lives somewhere transformed in the painting, for others to feel it. And thus that painted moment lasts for years and years.

This Moment in Time

It is four in the morning. I wake as if called, leave my bed, slide open the glass door, and step out onto the deck and into the moon-white night. Moonlight blanches the bushes of my garden in a milky sheen. Presence is everywhere, fairly singing in the pine boughs, fluttering in the eucalyptus, and winding round my bare ankles in unmistakable invitation. I dress and close the door on my world of comfort, sleep, relationship, and step into the cold-blue light of the now full moon and head to the beach.

This strange, reflected light disguises the familiar world. My eyes are everywhere deceived, but my feet know the path, and my ears are tuned to the roar of the surf. In the dark, I make my way, as surely as an animal down the dirt lane, across the field, down the path through the pampas reeds, across the board over the dry stream bed, along the path to the beach. Over the roiling black sea, the pale moon is riding on galloping blue clouds. Everything seems to be glorying in the other, water and moon and wind and tide. An ecstasy of motion, a marriage of matter and light.

In the dark, in the sea-roar, the moment presents itself. The rock, the falling leaf, the passing cloud, the premorning light shimmering across a satin sea—all this is invitation. The world offers itself. In its unbearable beauty, it opens itself, moment by moment, and I, the one with eyes, stare back.

My brain can be distracted by thoughts that drift like pages of yesterday's newspapers on the currents of dark alley winds. Thoughts, transient, remnants of the emptied-out events of the day, the unrealized tasks, the questions, the scratching, crossed out drafts of theories about the meaning of it all, and what after all, comes next?

I want to hold each precious moment and yet—so often—it seems that there's not enough time. Not enough time to notice each moment. To remember to pay attention. I'm constantly distracted by the buzzing cloud of worries. Too worried to live my life. Too worried to do what I need to do, too worried to drink in every bit of this place so I can carry it with me like water in a camel's hump, as I go on to whatever, in the dry and windy unknown, comes next. And what does come next?

Just look at the ocean. Follow the incoming waves. What comes next is what just passed: the next moment. Watching the sea is a good way to practice this. In the dark, I sit on the cliff's edge and look down at the incoming waves, lit by the light of the moon, curling white on the sand. Farther out, the waves, like time, smooth into each other on the way to the horizon. Swelling and expiring, waves are constant as breath, in and out. One after another, here and then gone. All part of the heave and swell of the never-ending sea of ever-renewing, always passing waves.

Sometimes when I'm walking on the beach at low tide, shining little tide pools are alive with bubbling anemones, those rubbery little disc-like creatures, opening and closing, reaching, and holding, breathing, in and out, as waves of foam come rolling in. Always nourishing. Never the same. They could be here forever, like the waves that roll in and bubble around my boots.

Writing those words, an image arises of Loren Eiseley, the great poet and paleontologist, walking out one similar early morning, on a similar Pacific Ocean beach after a storm. The waves were rolling in, tumbling, and churning, and the wind was whipping, stinging cold. Far down the beach, Eiseley spied a lone figure right at the place where the waves spill their load and the sea water floods up in arcs and then slides back, seeping into the sand.

As Eiseley got closer, he saw that the man was picking up starfish, cast up by the churning surf, where, stranded by the receding tide, without water, they would die. Eiseley approached the man and asked him why he was doing what he was doing when there were so many. And the waves were coming in so fast!

The man, wind whipping his slicker, said quietly, without stopping his work, "The stars throw well. One can help them."

The Joy of Dogs

This morning, because a muscle in my back is sore from pulling up weeds and cleaning—preparing for another dreaded batch of prospective buyers—instead of going as usual to my Casita, I took my coffee into a nice hot tub, where I opened a book by Ruskin about the laws of form in nature. Good thought to enliven the body for a run. "The beginning of all my own right artwork in life," he wrote, "depended not on my love of art, but of mountains and sea." Right, I thought, and read on until the water cooled, then put Ruskin back on the shelf, got dressed, put the coffee makings out for my beloved, and went out into the mist, to the source, to the sea.

I trotted along the newly paved road that curves down the hill toward the beach and was joined by a young black lab and his chocolate friend. The only company around that early, they set upon me with enthusiasm, leaping about, and nipping at my shoes.

"Well, come on!" I called, and they charged ahead, Hurray! A run! And we all turned the corner toward the beach. Low tide. Oh good.

The surf was silver and gray with long lines of low breaking waves. The black bones of Duxbury Reef reached out toward the distant lights of San Francisco. The shore was covered in glistening black rocks. The black lab charged into the silver light, sending shorebirds aloft in a twittering mass that circled low and settled on another fan of sand.

I slowed to a walk to better manage the uneven footing and watch my animal companions' freedom and unbounded joy. They chased each other, charged the birds, rampaged among the kelp, and brought me sticks to throw. I laughed at their happiness. Pure joy in being, in running, in rolling in the sand where some stinking dead thing moldered; pure joy in quarreling and fetching and pleading with me to throw some more sticks. Their animal joy, I was taught, was irrational, for they are not rational beings. But how do we know, really? We tend to minimize what we don't understand and doubt what we don't see. And yet, as the old Irish farmer said, chuckling, when a young tourist asked if he believed in the Little People or Fairies, "Nay, nay!" Haw haw haw! "But they're there anyway!"

When the dogs sped on ahead, I walked up near the cliff in relative silence and there, speaking of things we do not see but are there anyway, I discovered a geological process at work. The waves were crashing way out towards San Francisco, revealing a long shining stretch of dark, clay-like rock and tide pools. In the still air next to the cliff, I started to notice a tiny sound. It followed along beside me as I walked. I couldn't see what it was. The sound was so faint that it registered just above the sound of my breathing. A tiny little sound like rain. I looked around. Then up.

The cliff, normally so still and blond, with its occasional crags and no plants at all, was alive with movement. Pebbly shards of clay were tumbling down in rivulets, forming little alluvial fans at the base of the cliff. Erosion! Geology happening right before my eyes.

As I continued along in the shadow of the cliff, it was with a new respect for the immanence of change. Farther down the beach, the cliff top was edged with plants—coyote bushes, blackberry scrub, and a couple of grand Monterey cypresses. These great old trees cling to the earth, half their roots burrowing deep into the land and the others reaching out to the sky as if searching for their lost water. Thus poised, they will rest until years or storms can bring them down to where the waves and sun, over time, will sculpt them into something I, or someone else with aspirations to artistic greatness, might photograph. Meanwhile, erosion continues, breaking off bits and chunks of earth and sending them tumbling, breaking, clattering down the cliff. All of which feeds the beach and helps shape the wall of the cliff as a timeless looking, moving, changing thing.

Thinking of how the tiny little shards, in this moment barely visible, are shaping the ancient cliff, I wondered: *what if we could watch our aging, our wrinkles etching themselves into our clean faces? The putting on of weight? The progress of our bones giving way? Would we live differently? What if for a moment, the illusion of our Selves Eternal, as we can't help but think of ourselves, fell away and we could watch time move daily through our skin? Each night the days of our lives are reduced by one, the monks chant. Really knowing that, would we work faster? Think clearer? Finally dispense with the superfluous? How will I hold on to all that will, as sure as the sun will set, shift, move, change, sink into the darkness of memory, leaving me scrambling to capture each now, even as the dogs rush back and circle around my legs, panting and begging for sticks for me to throw into the surf for them to chase and return, again.*

Am I complaining? Not at this moment. When I get back to the house, I will grind the beans and make two coffees and bring them into the bedroom where my beloved awaits. Will I be complaining then? Not then. His face will be smiling and welcoming and the sun will be pouring in through the skylight. We will snuggle together with our mugs of hot, dark coffee and watch the hummingbirds outside the window dart after each other on the hanging feeder. One of us will start complaining later, for sure, about one thing or another, but the day, as just about every day, opens in happiness and mutual gratitude.

8

The Shadow

This blue and yellow spring morning trumpets its brilliance like a marching brass band. The sound of color fills the air—a wind-hiss high and near billows like silk over the lower tones of the distant ocean's roar. The sound stretches westward to the meadow and meets the sharp red notes of the rooster's crowing from across the mesa. All around, the air glitters with the sound of the chattering of the small brown birds that liven the bushes in the blackberry bog.

Just beyond the meadow, a small dog yaps. This would be Pandora, the Jack Russel terrier, who leaps, like something on a spring, straight up out of the waist-high grass and down again in pursuit of some doggy fancy. Thinking about her makes me smile. Dogs' lives here are full. Town dogs hang out. They lounge in lazy groups, like old men over stale coffee, or seals sunning themselves on the wooden walk that fronts the few town stores. When they've rested up or gotten a new idea, they'll go trotting down the road with companionable intent. Some wear bandannas. All have agendas.

Here this morning, through the open window where I sit in my Casita, the room breathes in, moving the crocheted curtain that covers the window, expanding and contracting like a dancer's ribcage, out and in, in sync with its partner, the shade cord. This curtain came from the fingers of my grandmother, and watching its tiny patterns pulls my mind back to summers in her dark, Victorian living room where she sat in her wing-back chair, and I sat on the floor watching her small hands wield the flashing silver needles. They flicked in and out, snagging and placing the white twine wound tight around her index finger. Also at her feet, beside the ball of twine, was the tattered workbook of patterns that promised many little squares of pixilated bears and rabbits to the patient and accurate follower of the codes. I remember a vague amazement that from the nothing that preceded the stitches, would come doilies, booties, tablecloths, and, her tour de force, a whole bedspread bearing my name. And now this little curtain hangs here, filtering out the brightest light. Do the fibers remember their origin? That closed, dark house with its old, unmoving air?

The big blue bird drops to the deck and screams. Jay! He screams his name again and hops down the steps on legs like sticks and flaps himself up to the birdbath. I have just filled the bath and the bird sips and dunks and flutters his wings like a kid in a plastic pool, banging the water just to see it splash. The sunlight around the birdbath glistens as he splashes. He screams again and flaps upward to the big pine's branch, leaving a contrail of glittering droplets as he goes. If you fill it, he will come. His enjoyment quiets my mind. Helps me recover from the strain of yesterday's meeting.

Yesterday, here in my little sanctuary, a woman sat opposite me on the window seat. She had come to have her portrait taken—a business enterprise I'm starting to cultivate to help get us out of our hole—and we were talking about where we might do it. Beach? Lagoon? Hillside? She was pale and still as a paper doll, composed, and so lacking in substance that I could imagine her passing through walls. Her beauty was such that she could pose for Ivory Soap cameos, hand creams, marble figurines. As we talked, I gazed out through the open glass door at the wind moving in the trees, the white clouds sifting over the blue sky. She looked past me to the wall of books. Happy in the nurturing presence of nature, momentary relief from the weeks of rain, I was thinking about how best to capture her beauty on film. Then, in case I hadn't missed it, she announced that she was depressed.

I asked if she wanted to talk about it.

"I don't think I am capable of surviving," she said.

It was a moment of dissonance, as if a great stone had been rolled back, revealing, behind the calm exterior, the contortion of her despair. As she began to speak, steepling and unsteepling her pale fingers, a cold, black, empty air seemed to suck in the very light of my room.

"I just don't find life interesting enough," she said. "If it came right down to it, there's just not enough here to make it worth the effort."

Coming from this beautiful, accomplished person who, to outward appearances had everything, it was a Faustian lament. As she went on, I felt myself drawn into her feeling, and a cloud of misery and failure began pressing, like a gray mass, down on my chest. I started to feel like a plane out of fuel, going in heavy circles, growing tired of my own voice, hearing myself matching her misery, talking about the sale of the house, what we'd do or couldn't do, or didn't know what to do. She listened without comment, and in her silence, my mood descended further until I realized that she was encouraging my recitation as if that gave her permission for her own. Or was it the reverse?

I looked outside. Sunlight was surging over the sea of greens and golden color was rustling in the willow and alder boughs. Leaves were budding in the sweet round tree and clouds puffed over the shining Eucalyptus leaves. Yellow acacia blossoms were glistening on the wind. I withheld a surge of grief—not for this troubled woman, or even myself, but for the sweetness of life itself, everything innocently living and budding, doing its best and being met with our ingratitude or worse, our indifference.

I asked her, very cautiously, what things she could think of that gave her pleasure. She thought a long time. There was an afternoon at a lake back in the fall. "But I can't go there every day." Then, looking around, she added, "And I don't live in a beautiful place." I did not say, all no doubt true, but *all in your point of view*.

Instead, I said, offering the best I could think of, "There's always the sky. When there's nothing else, isn't there? The beautiful blue sky, like today?"

And with a barely tolerant half smile, she said, "But I've seen blue sky. Is that really a reason to get up in the morning? To see another blue sky?"

I have studied blue sky for years, trying to render it in paint, in film, in silver, now words. Sky is never the same. You think you have it down, and then you look and, no. Not even close. Look at it now: that Giotto blue sky, with those brilliant little horizontal clouds that go from nearly white to pale cerulean. This sky today is alive with residual glow from the setting full moon. But is this enough? If it were just a color overhead, I guess I could see her point. But this light is like a being. Scintillating. Life-giving. I watch it. I praise it. I breathe it in.

This sky, this moment, will never, ever be there again. And I know that too. I tried to tell her that. Again, her sad, tolerant smile.

"Such a thin thread holds me in life," she said. "Nothing has any juice."

I suggested we go downtown, to the beach, for the picture. I was thinking we would see all sorts of people downtown, fortunate and unfortunate. Maybe she'd be lifted by some perspective. Or at least some lunch.

Downtown

Downtown. The word is somewhat an exaggeration for this ramshackle assortment of worn-out wood frame shops, a one-pump gas station, a Western movie-style bar, a café, a sweet little museum, a has-all general store, and a fishing dock. In the summer, it's a typical beach town. In the winter, it just looks dirty. Overnight, parked cars turn brown from the dust that rushes in swirls down the two-block stretch of the main street. Skateboarders weave in and out of the gritty columns, and pickup trucks slalom around and behind them. Muscular dogs bounce in the flat beds, barking insults to their comrades on the wooden sidewalks. Street-dogs, in their excitement, bound over each other and scatter to the sidelines, mobs of giggling, barefoot children. Sparrows flutter in the dirt pools. Here, even new shoes, much less new faces, look old.

If you glance around, you'll see that everybody wears old clothes here. Old, as in from a long time back. Silky, tie-dyed, see-through things on top and bottom, headbands with long trails, Isadora Duncan scarves entwined with waist-length locks. Necklaces here can be made of anything: feathers, teeth, rocks, even—seen once on a bare-chested man coming out of the laundromat—a live boa constrictor. Living fur is stylish too; I once saw, at the cash register of the general store, crawling out of the milk-white cleavage of a black-haired young girl, an actual, live, brown mouse.

One day recently, I was downtown shopping for some meat. I said to Bert, the butcher behind the counter in the general store, which has been there over a hundred years—wooden floors, open beam ceiling, rafters draped in spiders' webs, flies buzzing everywhere—"Wow, what a good-looking shirt." He beamed. Blue eyes, fleshy face, thinning blonde hair, middle-age gut, the canonical butcher in his bloody butcher's apron.

"You like it?"

"I do."

He said, "You know, I've been thinking about shirts lately. Since I moved here from the Midwest, I haven't bought any clothes. Even Levis are so much more expensive here, I just won't buy 'em. So I found some dockers at Kmart, and some tee shirts, and I've been wearing them ever since. But yesterday, I decided to go to Petaluma and thought maybe I'd get a haircut. And the barber was wearing a shirt like this. So I went on down to Kmart and bought one."

"It looks good."

I told him that if I were taking a photograph of The Proper Butcher Today, he'd be perfect. Just the right blue shirt. Just the right blood-spattered apron, just the right blue cap.

"Yeah, the cap," he said. "I used to wear that black cap, but you know, I'm just not a black cap guy. I bought this blue one last week."

With his big, open, Midwestern face, Bert's good looking. And interesting. He wrapped up my naked chicken. When I took the brown package to the counter, a thin, bearded man with bright blue eyes stepped up to the counter and smiled. "Chicken?"

"Chicken," I said.

"Well, that'll cure the existential dread."

I walked away smiling.

At the cash register by the door, I signed the worn yellow card with the free-hand-drawn lines underneath the names and wished the owner's nephew, a young, studious guy who came to help on weekends, a happy day.

Then, out into the sunshine, I stepped around a couple of lounging dogs and made my way, boots clomping, down the wooden boardwalk to my car. That's when I noticed that the sky was an amazing blue. Just like Bert's shirt. Reaching my car, I gazed for a moment at the gritty street scene with the echoing wooden boardwalk, the dogs, the dust, the barefoot kids, and the tie-dyed oddballs and aging hippies and outcasts and occasional normal people all shuffling along in the morning light, and I smiled. Then, feeling a bit peckish, as the English say, I went into the café. The tired-faced owner, whose name was Cindy, welcomed me. "Your enchilada will be right up." She knew what I liked.

I sat down at my favorite table by the woodstove and took a book from the shelf and opened to some poems. I heard the owner holler into the kitchen to tell her daughter that the enchilada was for me.

"Right," came the reply from the steamy interior, "light on the cheese and no sour cream?"

"Right." Soon a blue Fiestaware plate was before me, framing a steaming enchilada—perfect, as always.

When Cindy handed down my bill, I reached into my pocket. Empty! Whoops. "Can I bring you a check this afternoon?" I asked.

"Oh sure," she said, with casual smile. "Whenever!" I thought of my mother. Try getting her enchilada on credit on 57th street.

We brought my proud New York mother here once, after we were first married, to enjoy the house and our new life. We wanted to show her the quaint little town, the beautiful landscape, and give her a sense of the freedom, the possibility open to all of us here in the West. We wanted her to love the place. We took her downtown to the café. Cindy was at her most gracious, "So you've brought your mother, eh! We'll try not to scare her!"

It was early on Sunday, and the town was pretty quiet. Still, we were nervous. In her frilly silk blouse and perfect Chanel suit and Ferragamo shoes, my mother looked like someone from another world—which she was. She studied the hand-drawn menu on the chalkboard as if to see which of the choices would be least hazardous to her health.

Accustomed to fine dining, my mother did not trust "atmosphere." In fact, she rarely ventured from her roost on the corner of 57th and Sixth Avenue, and when she did, the country was not what she sought. "Country," to her, growing up in Silver Spring, Maryland, a suburb of Washington D.C., was a condition to escape, a term of derision. "I hate all this nature," I heard her say as we drove through the eucalyptus forest on the way into town. "All those animals eating each other. Do you have those deadly ticks here?"

On this first visit we were nervous. We wanted her to know we were doing well. We wanted her to understand why we loved it here. We took her to the old prairie-style church on the hill and then brought her "downtown" for breakfast. The café, dark and seasoned, looked as though it had been the same inside for fifty years, but the breakfast was as good as breakfast gets. Spicy sausage, pancakes—classic. Amazingly enough, Mother was happy. She ate her omelet, asked for a little more coffee, smiled at the waitress. We were all relieved.

Leaving the café full of warm good will, we strolled down the dusty wooden walkway and all piled into the Lexus, which was parked nose-in, facing the general store. Mother, riding in the front, was being daintily complimentary about the town, talking about how the locals seemed friendly and how all the place really needed was a coat of paint—when screams broke out behind us.

A tall, lanky, wild-haired, town drunk in dusty clothes and a wide-brimmed black hat was attacking a strange new drunk who was kicking Bear, the round, orange dog whose temperament seemed the same as his name. Bear belonged to the black-hatted man, who shared him—along with who-knows-what-else—with a small, youngish street woman, who, thankfully, was nowhere to be seen. As the two drunks fought, other street characters piled on. In the ensuing brawl, Bear yelped and howled, the men yelled and pummeled each other, and their bodies blurred behind us in a cloud of thrashing dust.

Eager to get my mother away, my husband revved the engine and started inching back in reverse, and the men disbursed, flinging curses over their shoulders at each other. With my mother staring straight ahead like Queen Elizabeth in her coach, the reversing car disbursed the fray. As we headed out of town, I turned back briefly, watching the tall, black-hatted man retreat, with Bear at his side, and wondered about the woman, his companion.

Mariah

I first noticed this woman, who called herself Mariah, in the street in front of the grocery on a Saturday night months before. It was pouring down rain. It was dark. I'd just pulled up to the curb, again in front of the store, to get some last-minute milk before they closed. In the space beside my car was an odd sight. At first, I thought the thing in the puddle was a dead animal. It was a big, black form that looked like a bearskin or some kind of artificial, hairy-thing coat. Then, just as I was studying the puddle, a white BMW slid into the parking space on the other side of it and a sleek blonde woman in a black vinyl raincoat and knee-high Hunter boots stepped out. She gazed at the shape in the mud in horror.

"Oh, honey," she cried in dismay. "Oh, Mariah, honey, get up!"

The woman reached out her gloved hand, but did not touch the disgusting, heaving mass. Slowly, the coat rose, and from underneath it emerged a bloody, terrible face, eyes red and blurred, half shut, lips swollen and bleeding, circled by brown hair the consistency of the animal coat. The wretched woman wove unsteadily and then crumbled back down into the mud. The "Beemer" woman, cool as a statue of the Virgin Mary, reached to support her, but Mariah just flailed her fur-covered arms and muttered some guttural curses and the woman stood back to avoid being splattered.

As she turned to the front of the store, looking around for help, a tall, surly man in cowboy boots, with a wide brimmed black hat, loped into the scene and stood over the figure in the animal coat, who was still struggling in the mud. Rain drained from his brim onto her as he looked down. She stretched out her hand. The cowboy curled his lip and cursed, flicked a cigarette ash—not exactly on her but not exactly away from her either—and slouched on off into the night. The fur-covered form slumped back into the mud. The well-dressed woman went up to the grocery and I followed, as that's where I was going. Inside, the woman asked if anyone had phoned 911. Bert, in his blue shirt, already in the doorway, said, with a sad face, that he'd done that. Everyone stood around shaking their heads. Apparently, this had happened before.

I'd never seen anyone face down in the mud. I'd never seen a woman with a face like raw hamburger, bleeding. But I'd lived in big cities and, like many prosperous women on their own, I was spooked by the image of the "bag lady," with her shopping cart piled high with the reeking load of her worldly goods, crossing a busy street in Manhattan. No matter how prosperous or secure, it seems that deep down in the basement of the psyche where fear coils round itself there dwells this mental "bag lady" who can haunt us with the image of the most abject, unthinkable failure. "Don't want to end up as a bag lady!" I'd heard well-dressed women joke, for to most of us, having never seen real hardship up close, it was a joke—but not really funny. Nor did I feel anything even close to humor as I stepped around the mud-soaked woman and went into the store.

For a moment, I stood by the door with the group watching beside the "Beemer" woman. I didn't know her, but I knew who she was. She was single, rich, early middle age, a little older than I. Standing in the rain with the others, waiting for the EMTs to come, we shared a certain anonymous camaraderie.

"Why do you think this happens to people?" she asked no one in particular.

"She clearly needs help," I said. "Can't someone do something?"

"You can't save someone who doesn't want to be saved," said the butcher.

"Well, that'll be her," someone else said.

Watching with the others, I felt an inexpressible sorrow. How did they know what the poor woman wanted or didn't want, or what circumstances, inner or outer, had pushed her over the edge? I'd seen her once, with my own eyes, call to the universe to be saved. It was last summer when we were starting to talk about selling our house. I was standing in front of the real estate office and was about to pull open the door and step in when I heard a shout and looked across the street.

There, in the sunlight, in front of the garage, stood a small, tanned, erect, barefoot woman of indeterminate age in a calf-length denim skirt with a thin, long-sleeved pink blouse. Big sunglasses, little leather shoulder purse. The skirt and the blouse blew against her thinness in the wind. She stood with grace inside the clothes. She stood upright, as if somewhere inside her there was a chord of integrity that, surrounded by different habits, perhaps different chemical makeup, different partners, or different everything, might have made her a star. But then she turned and I saw her face, red and ravaged, probably ruined by alcohol and whatever other addictions sustained her. Mariah.

Just as I was about to dismiss her as another sad case, she raised her arms and opened her mouth and from somewhere deep down in her lower chakras came a glorious, full-colored voice, belting out the opening bars of "Amazing Grace." Passers-by stopped and stared as she sang. I was holding open the door of the real estate office. I had to wipe tears from my face before going in.

Attitude Adjustment

The amazing thing about grace is how it comes, by surprise, from the strangest sources and sometimes is so subtle that we can miss it if we're not awake. This morning, for instance, my waking prayer to the Universe was "Get me out of here!" I'd had it with money problems, house problems, his problems. Circular problems with no solution. Which car shall we take now that it's raining? The one that leaks so bad we have to bail her out? Or the one with no windshield wipers? Have you emptied the buckets in your office yet? What are we going to do with the two-inch gap in the roof that we've just discovered is letting rain pour straight down between the facia and the kitchen wall? Plug it up with invoices we can't afford to pay? *Final demand.* Ha ha ha! *Get me out of here.*

As I stood in the kitchen pouring boiling water over the aromatic, freshly ground coffee beans, I found my mind drifting down its well-worn road into memories of affluence, back in the days when my career was flourishing, though my personal life was anything but. This time, I am coming out of Bergdorf Goodman's and heading down 57th Street with my mother, toward Bendel's. The time is ten years ago, before I dreamed of moving west. I had just purchased two little solid silver candlesticks. Four hundred dollars apiece. My mother loves Bergdorf's, but as we walk away, she is very quiet. I say, "A divorce is a traumatic thing. It's important that I not feel poor."

She says, "It's important that you not *get* poor." *Ha ha.*

We laugh then and decide to cross over and take a turn through Bendel's, "just to look." It is Christmas and nowhere are the decorations more opulent than in Henri Bendel's. Just cross the threshold into Bendelland and your brain cells start doing cartwheels from the combination of perfumes and twinkling lights and glittering bottles and shining ribbons and bows and things, things, things, all heavenly and exactly what you need in order to feel the way you want to feel—beautiful, pampered, desirable—happy! And why not? As the ads say: *You deserve it!* By the time you leave, though, if you have passed unscathed through the furies of desire, what's left of your brain cells are twitching. In that state, we make it to the door, exit into the cool air of the street, still laughing. No additional bags, no additional guilt, we decide to go down to the corner and across the street to Wolf's deli for lunch. They have skyscraper-high sandwiches. Pickles that are a meal in themselves. All for $9.95. Even in the eighties, that was cheap.

"What are you going to do now?" my mother asks as a massive plate is put down before her. "I mean, really?"

Yum, yum. What a good sandwich. Waitress, could I have a few hundred more? So I can just keep eating this sandwich forever and not have to answer her, or myself, now or ever, that terrible question.

What? Do? Who knew?

"Oh, now I can do exactly what I want to do," I say. "No one's holding me back. It's the right thing. I know it."

"And where are you going to live?" Munch, munch. "Why don't you just try New York for a while. Surely it would be better for your business." Munch, munch, munch. "You can live with me..."

Gulp. She means well. But.

"I need to be in the land. That's all I know."

"But what does that mean?"

"I don't know."

I had my visions of Thoreau in his cabin in the woods. Or of Edward Abbey in his cabin in the desert. A meaningful life. Watching plants, counting mice, getting to know the spiders by name. Ruminating on metaphysical ideals. Walking a lot. But I couldn't tell her that. I didn't know how to explain what I was looking for without her thinking me an airhead. Perhaps if I had put it in a religious context she would have understood. If I'd spoken in terms of Saint Francis of Assisi—communing with birds, animals, renouncing worldly concerns, all for religious purposes—that would have been fine. A religious intention she would have approved of, at least theoretically. Even Thoreau, she would tolerate. But she would not have been able to find a place in her mind for the destitution such a lifestyle could bring on, in the nineties, in the dusty backroads of coastal California, such as where I was now.

Now, waking "in the land"—my own land, as it happens—and a poverty quite un-Franciscan, I was anything but serene. Today, I hated everything. My damn roses always staring up at me, needing pruning. My damn lemon tree always needing water. My damn bushes, my damn grass, the whole damn tsunami wave of blackberries threatening to engulf the house. I'm in the land all right. My kitchen is about to be in the land, too, when this wall rots and falls down. Get me out of here!

In this mood, I went down to my Casita—which I also hated, sitting as it does, so neat and pretty, accusing me of all I do not accomplish. Damn. Damn. I rounded the corner on the path by the rock roses, and right in front of the Casita, in the little garden, by the birdbath stood a doe.

I stopped.

She raised her head.

I spoke.

She looked at me.

I took a tiny step closer.

She flicked her ear.

I explained to her that I had to get by her to go up the steps and into the studio, but she didn't seem inclined to move. When I approached the steps she eased back, the way a member of a crowd does to let someone important pass. Then, as I inched closer, I noticed she had only three legs.

"Oh, it's you!" I said, in wonder.

I'd seen her before from a distance. The left rear leg had been all but severed at the knee, from which it dangled, rotten and tarry. Somewhere thereafter, that ruined appendage had apparently dropped off, and the stump had healed. She let me pass by her, step up to the deck, go inside.

On my desk, I had an apple. Not from the tree in my garden but from the store, as it was spring. I brought it down, held it out to her. She stretched her head closer. Curious? Hungry? I knelt down, rolled the apple gently toward her, and she made a little hop-step toward me and took it.

Deer do not do that.

The heart of a deer is pure and wild. Unlike raccoons that do their song and dance up at the house at dinnertime, deer do not beg. Oh, they will help themselves to your roses—if you are so careless as to leave them unfenced. But only the blossoms. And only then if you're not around. Deer, in their wildness, are sufficient in themselves. Perhaps why the ancient Celts put their image on ceremonial bowls.

Not only did this little doe take my apple, but she stayed, rolling the apple around on her long pink tongue, regarding me with calm. Looking into her eyes, at close range, I felt a sudden stillness. A kind of peace. As if I were in the presence of someone whose infinite gentleness comes from long accepting pain. I sat on my step; she munched her apple. I let the moment sink in.

A Jungian analyst I know would say of this moment, "When nature presents you a Gift, unwrap it." For nature, like dreams, he would say, speaks in the language of visual detail. In dream language, this doe, my gender mate, would represent my Shadow, and hold a mirror to a part of me I can't or do not want to see. And what is that?

I thought of that dangling, rotted leg. When it would no longer hold her, did she dread losing it? As I may dread being separated from a past that could not hold me. Or a present I cannot sustain? And did she try, now and then, to lean on it, that dead leg, even when it wasn't there, and did it hurt? As I hurt now, looking back? Looking forward? And how did she heal? Did she have to struggle to scrape the dead limb free before the deadness could spread throughout her and bring her down? How did she wrench it free? All those bones. Sinews.

Things that should have held together but could not. I know, I know, I said to her. I let a whole leg of my life go, and I cried for years over that, and now I cry when the new life I've chosen cannot seem to hold up. Will I ever know anything?

Choice. Being deer in the wild, her choices are limited, clear. Being human, my choices are multiple, tangled, complex. In the past, I could get out of anything. Hail a cab. Board a train. Take a flight to an opposite coast. Now, I am crippled, but only if I choose to look at it that way. The car needs brakes, and I can barely afford gas. But I have a car, don't I? The doe, having finished her apple, glanced up at me, then hobbled, unhurried, off into the brush.

Of Wild Men and Hardworking Animals

When life serves them hardship, they do not whine or complain. They do not ponder their worth. They do not question their reason for being. They don't have jobs but always manage to support themselves. They do what they're outfitted to do. They are resourceful to the full extent of their species—and perhaps beyond. I saw this in action once, earlier this winter.

It was late at night, and the security light went on, and I decided to have a look at whatever was moving around outside. Up by the road, in the blaze of light, a big, muscular raccoon, not one of our regular visitors, but clearly one used to working for a living, was practicing his trade craft on the garbage bin. Standing on his haunches, with his delicate fingers gripping the lid, he tipped the can onto its side. The lid, bound by bungee cords, stayed on. No problem.

He pushed the can gently with his clever little hands, rolling it slightly. Still the top stayed on. He checked it, fingering around the rim, tugging slightly. Then rolled it some more; checked the lid. Still tight. Rolled it some more; checked it. Still tight. He rolled it and checked it until the bin had made the complete circle. Then he sat back on his fat little haunches and considered, while I, from my window, considered him: he was not a ransacker, nor a marauder, as raccoons are often miscredited to be.

He was more like a safe-cracker—thoughtful, deliberate, with a built-in burglar's mask. Finally, having reached the limit of his tolerance for mystery, he rose once more and pushed the bin a foot or two, and then, meeting with no success, brushed himself off and waddled on down the road into the dark.

Raccoons bow to no one. However, they know their place. A few months ago, in the summer, at the end of a roast lamb dinner, the visiting dear friend who cooked the meal surprised us afterward by filling a kettle full of scrapings and bones and announcing that the viscous glop would become soup. Alas, she left before accomplishing the transformation. So I stashed the kettle to the back of the fridge and ignored it for a decent period of time, like you do with leftovers, unable to just throw them away, until finally, when they are covered in green fur and you feel justified, you heave them out. But I did not do that with this kettle of glop. Instead, one night, as a sort of science experiment, I put the whole kettle out on the deck for the animal kingdom to discover, wondering, *Who, in the Wild, eats Soup?*

Darkness had fallen when I noticed Rocky Raccoon hunched over the pot. Raccoons, you may have observed if you live in the woods or anywhere near garbage bins, have an interesting way of moving. They carry their weight not in their feet, as other four-legged folk do, but in their curving spines. So they seem to move like things on wire, never plunking down, but always swaying around, hovering over a thing. So Rocky was swaying over the pot, reaching in with his spidery hands and feeding himself—as we would, if we had no spoons—in a kind of drippy, sloppy way. When he finally latched upon a hunk of substance, he wheeled away, snarling to the others of his kind who were emerging from the shadows, to hunker and chew his morsel in the periphery of the light.

Enter the skunk. In case you've been wondering where the skunk lies in the hierarchy of the food chain, here's how it goes. Assuming that Soup is at the bottom, and Cat has abandoned the scene, Rocky—and he was as surprised to learn this as I—is not at the top. He learned this sad fact by watching from the periphery of the deck, as we were watching from inside the house, as a silky black creature with a magisterially plumy, black, white-striped tail waddled right up to the pot and sank his narrow little snout down in to slurp. The skunk.

Rocky was visibly disconcerted. He moved in carefully to sniff the amazing intruder. The skunk pivoted—without diverting the activities of his front end (neat and pointed, unencumbered by excess brain)—so that his rear end faced Rocky square on. Surprise and amazement registered in the clever Raccoon's eyes. He leaned forward to sniff the potent area. Then instantly drew back, blinking. Irresistibly, he reached a forepaw out to almost . . . almost touch the fascinating stranger. He seemed to sense (and I knew) that never had he been so close to total devastation.

As we watched, the skunk calmly, with all the confidence of a bearer of nuclear arms, slurped and slurped and the level of liquid in the pot went down inch by inch. While his front end was focused on the meal, his rear end, with its signal black-and-white striped tail, remained erect as a warning flag to Rocky and all comers of dangerous consequence to any interruption. When Rocky moved forward, in the socially understood "that's enough, now my turn" swagger, the skunk jigged a bit on his hind legs and flicked the aromatic tail. Rocky backed off. I edged the glass door shut. In his own time, the skunk took his last slurp, lifted his head, shook it a bit and left.

I think our cats, Lily and Old Yellow Cat, were gratified. So often in their lives had Rocky hindered their own illusions of universe mastery. Now, at last, he was put in his place. Nature's way is always to seek balance. In the end, on our deck, no one pushed anyone over the edge, everyone got a share in the soup, I got rid of it without guilt, and we all learned something new about getting along.

Writing these words, I feel a chill at the back of my neck. My beloved and I argued again yesterday. It was a rainy afternoon. The latest offer on the house had fallen through—buyer who seemed so perfect couldn't get financing—sending us into a tailspin. I wanted my smart husband to come up with some new, alternate plan. He turned on me in anger.

"Is that what you're waiting for? Some magic plan? There is no magic plan!"

"But we can't just sit here!"

Then he exploded.

"Fine, you want to make a plan? Fine. Go ahead."

And he grabbed his car keys, stormed out, slammed his car door, and peeled away in a cloud of gravel and dust.

I stood alone in the ringing silence

I thought of "The Hole." The great omen. The hole in the road we went into when we first met, that he loved so much. Omen of what? We were in it now, for sure. Up to our necks. What happens if we can't pull out of this tailspin in time? I thought of my father's words, "Never get foreclosed!" But how could we figure all this out if we kept spinning into rows every other moment?

I put on the kettle to boil water for coffee and remembered a scene, back in this room, when we first moved into this house. My father had come to visit, for the first and only time, so see me and my new husband in our new life. We'd planned everything carefully to make the visit perfect for him, but within an hour of his arrival, my beloved and I were in a twister after I suggested varying the plan and he wanted to stick to the original, or something like that, something normal people would deal with in two sentences, but there we were, going at it like dogs and cats until I stormed out of the house in desperate frustration.

My father, standing on the deck, admiring the view, looked almost amused as I rushed by. Then, probably seeing I was serious, called after me, "Hey, wait!"

I stopped at the car, opened the door, looked at him, thinking, *try and stop me!*

"Hey, hey, wait a minute. Hold on," he said, hurrying over to lean on the open door.

"Look," he said, looking down at me with his big smile. "He's just raving because he thinks you don't hear him. I know you hear him. But he just keeps yelling. I don't know why. But I know he's crazy about you. So, relax." He grinned and gave my shoulder a little shake, the way he would a fine suit jacket on a hanger. "And really," he said in a low voice, "take it from me. You don't want to end up alone."

I had to smile back at him. My father knew a thing or two about arguing and quite a lot about ending up alone. He was a keen judge of people, and he liked my husband. ("He's a nice man!") So, I unclenched myself. Then, after a moment of thought, he said, "Ya know, he's probably just as scared as you are!"

Now, as I worried for my dear husband out in the fog on the dangerous, treacherous coastal roads and I waited to hear the grind of tires on the gravel, my father's words sat with me, and I remembered all the goodness of my poor, beleaguered fellow. We were caught in an emotional dynamic that neither one of us had the skill to resolve, and having our house on the market, our home always subject to the scrutiny of prospective buyers, just made it worse. We hated the prospective buyers, but we needed them, and we hated that we needed them. But we loved each other and always forgave each other. Remembering that calmed me down.

I thought about that movie with the sappy message. How wrong it was! Love is *not* "never having to say you're sorry." Love is *always* having to say you're sorry. Which I did, instantly, when he appeared in the door, soggy with rain, holding out flowers.

Liver Chi Backup

Each morning I wake wondering if this is the day on which the ground will crack open and swallow up my life and all the tables and chairs in it. Today, as always, I open my eyes carefully, the way a frog's eyes blink up out of the muck. I check out the scene through the windows. All is well. The stars are still hung there where I left them yesterday. In the sky over the ridge are the blinking lights of the six o'clock flight from Seattle, in which people are putting up their tray tables, taking off their glasses, readying their feet to return to Earth at SFO. Outside the east window, the eucalyptus crowns are waving, raucous with arguing crows. Far off, across the north meadow, the rooster announces another morning having safely arrived.

Today the sky is clear. We've had so much rain. All week I've been feeling like the rain. Illness and rain. Nothing seemingly diagnosable, just a persistent stitch in the left side and general sense of malaise. Yesterday I went to see the local acupuncturist, Sunflower, a name I suspect she was not born with. She is tall and thin with long yellow hair and a translucent beauty in her shadowy sky-blue eyes. Though thin, she carries her body with a quiet sense of precious weight as if she had gold bars dangling underneath her heavy sweatshirt. Her feet, in shearling booties, are silent on the oriental rug. She moves with awareness. No wasted steps. No disruptive surprises. She has the bearing of someone who had earned her wisdom through suffering.

Independent-minded, she holds her practice not in the medical offices in the city but in a small hut in a redwood glade on some property she owns outside of town. The hut seems, like many structures in the area, handbuilt—but by elves. It's very small, no larger than my Casita, round, with driftwood door frames and natural wood siding and a sort of domelike, cedar shake roof. Inside the hut is warmed by a tiny wood-burning stove and candles. She has one small desk, on which a seated Buddha, the size of a grapefruit, seems to preside, alongside a bound journal for her notes. Underneath, on shelves, she stashes her acupuncturist's apparatus. Beside the desk she has a handmade, sculpted wood chair, and in the center of the room stands the standard massage therapist's table. I entered the hut, put my bag down by the door, and smiled.

Sunflower greeted me with her usual reserve. Kind, but not gooey. Friendly, but not presumptuous. Watchful, but not rude. After the required pleasantries, I sat up on her table, and she pushed back my shirtsleeve and held my wrist to count the pulses. She looked up, her eyes searching mine.

"So what's going on?"

"I'm tired," I said. "There's this nagging pain."

"Right," she said. "Well, let's have you lie down."

I stretched out on her table. I dreaded the needles, but I trusted the healing form, so I did some deep breaths and waited to see what unsuspecting part of my body she'd aim for first, hoping it was not the feet.

"So how's that good-looking husband doing?"

She always asked this. He'd seen her once, for relaxation. He liked her.

"He's working on his company, but nothing's got any traction yet,"

"You still trying to sell the house?" People in town can't help but keep track of everything that's going on. Especially with what's going on with outsiders, as we were, and anyone else who hasn't lived there for fifty years.

I said the house was still for sale. People coming in. Looking around. Pain in the butt, really. She made a sound of acknowledgment and turned away to collect her needles.

I wondered, as she took my foot in both hands and probed for the point between the big toe and the first, what the foot had to do with pain in my right side. She inserted the needle.

"Ow!" A white branch of blazing energy shot through me.

"Sorry."

"What's that?"

"It's what we call 'Liver chi backup,'" she said.

"But my liver's on the other side, isn't it?"

"In Chinese medicine, we don't think literally," she said. "The liver channel is a particular energy channel. So, we're thinking about releasing stagnant energy in that channel that seems blocked."

"What causes that?"

"Repressed anger, for one thing. You know, liver, bile... it's a condition we often see with women."

"Figures," I said, glumly.

"So . . ." she smiled, "Any repressed anger going on?"

"Ha," I said, closing my eyes and heaving a big, acupuncture sigh. I could feel prickles of energy radiating up my spine.

In a sleepy voice, I told her I didn't like the situation we were in. She went, *um hum*. Between needle stabs and deep breaths, I told her I was sick of the constant flare-ups. Ridiculous arguments. *Um hum*. As she stuck in the needles, I followed the path of insertion and imagined my body as a map for my mind's complaints. So many complaints! What was the complaint that was driving this physical pain? What was its name? Grief? Dread? Rage? Blame?

"Ow!" I felt the needle pain almost as a condition of being.

"Sorry," she said again.

"I guess I have some anger," I said.

"There's a lot of it around," she said.

Normally, at this point in a session, she would bestow on me her ancient—she was probably in her forties—Buddha's smile. But today her face was blank. When I asked how things were going in her life, she turned away, doing something or other with her needles. Then she said that her German shepherd dog, Ariel, a beautiful creature known for his wit and intelligence, had just been shot and killed by a neighboring rancher's foreman. She said the man knew the dog was hers, but shot him anyway. The dog's sin? Venturing across the property boundary onto the rancher's land. I thought of my spider. Winced. Sunflower's pain, as she said this, cut through her usual professional reserve. Her tone was raw and dark and faded into a sort of untouchable desolation.

"I lost my best friend," she said. The way she said it made me wonder: *what about her husband?*

Then, as she returned to the table and held my wrist and listened for the new pulses, I sunk into a soft pillow of sleep and sorrow. Sorrow for the healer bereft of her dog and whatever made her need him so and sorrow for me and my own stupid dilemma. She looked down at me from the curtain of her long, straight hair and smiled, a true smile this time.

"Don't be sad. Sometimes we can't change what happens. But we can try to change our attitudes. This nice acupuncture should help."

Yes. The acupuncture helped. This morning, as I wake, I remember her, the care with which she treated my condition, while suffering deep pain of her own, and I feel the grace of her gift. And now, all I see around me is what I love. And I move into the day.

I leave the warm bed and go up the steps, behind the tail high, hungry cat, into the kitchen, make my coffee, and fill her dish, very quietly, so not to wake the sleeping man. Then, coffee cup in hand, camera hanging from my shoulder, I sneak outside like a thief in the night, someone on borrowed time, for the Casita.

The morning welcomes me. Clouds of little birds liven the dark brush as I pass. In the soft new light, my garden is bejeweled in a glittery gauze of dew. The little apple tree beams like a child in a pageant, playing the part of the sun. Tiptoe, reach high, circle the arms: smile. Click. Is it enough? Everything just as it is?

Is it enough? Have I captured the moment? The now? Safe, to have, for always? Everything just as it is? This lovely now? Never to change?

No wind, no sound, just light. On the twig of the plum tree, a little brown bird. Not chirping, not fluttering, not pecking or scratching at seed. Just still, in this moment of silence and light. Is the bird pondering his future, wondering if his song is inadequate? Or is he just paused in that still place between past and future, somewhere on the arc between lift and step, between inhale and exhale, just being.

Perhaps he is simply greeting the moment, doing the bird equivalent of *Ommmm*. I want to learn his stance. And I realize, a greeting, whether hello or goodbye, requires that the hand lets go to wave.

9

A Word about Sparrows

In the East, nobody gets excited about sparrows. Who wouldn't rather watch a brilliant red cardinal or hear the clarion cry of the eastern blue jay? Nothing like that here. Here I have the no-class scrub jay, who screams his name, bounces about, looks for trouble, and the crows. Here the crows fly in gangs and set up raucous parties in the pines, mobbing sleeping owls just for the fun of it. I haven't seen any ravens, but I'm told they're around. Their voice is deeper than the crows. When you see one, you'll know it right away. When little birds see one, they fade into the bushes. But aside from fat little quail, what I mostly have around my place are the little brown birds, the nondescript sparrows. How dull, I thought, at first. Now I am ashamed of my haughty, shallow ignorance.

To distinguish among our little brown birds is like learning to savor a subtle California spring. Unimpressive at first, but with myriad nuances that blossom into the inimitable flavor of the place. A cloud of sparrows is a gathering of distinctions. How to know them? I need to focus. There's more to learn, but here's what I know:

First, the white-crowned sparrow. He has the gray breast and the pink bill, as opposed to the white-throated sparrow who has the black bill and white throat. This little guy, says my bird book, has a "clear pensive" whistle, while the white-crowned sparrow has a "clear plaintive" whistle. There is also, somewhere around, a golden-crowned sparrow, but he "prefers denser shrubs," and I see him at my feeder infrequently. He should be happy here, though, for what could be denser than these blackberry thickets that surround my Casita on two sides.

The proud young tree beside the deck of my Casita, which, as a sapling, I freed from blackberries, is now beginning to thrive. Today it holds the bird feeder and usually at least one or two birds. Now, for the first time, its buds are bulging on its little branches. It looks like a fruit tree. Is it an apple? I'll have to wait till autumn to see—if I'm here. The thought makes me wonder: *Will the dreaded people who buy this house care for this tree? Will they even see it?* All these little individual birds, all these happily flowering trees, all these struggling plants are filled with the presence of my tending them. *What will they be when I'm gone?* In one way, no doubt, just fine. Nature is smarter than we are. But in some other way, when I bring my camera to them, when I am quiet, they show themselves to me. I see them. They are received.

All are part of the world of my attention. And does that matter? Once, a wise man and master photographer, whose work I was studying, said to me, when we were looking out at a scene of wild nature under threat from the consequences of civilization, "He needs our help." I think he meant the divine presence that enlivens all creation. I know he meant that seeing matters. Being present is a start.

After the "crowned" sparrows, the book tells me, there is a class of "streaked" sparrows. My favorite of these is the fox sparrow. A fat little fellow with lovely mahogany coloring, he is first to appear when I come down the path, and he perches near the feeder, watching as I pour in the seed. He is plump and round and striped and goes about kicking up the dead leaves in the dirt. The book says his song is brilliant and musical. Maybe. I've not yet been able to discern whose song is whose.

A little more streamlined than the fat fox sparrow is the song sparrow. He has a concentration of black feathers just under his chin. Very perky and dapper. I can pick him out best when looking through field glasses. Even from twenty feet away, this is the best way to see birds. You change your perspective. Get into their space without being intrusive. Your obtrusive self disappears. Then you can see the designs, markings, and patterns that make each bird unique. This is important. Observing sparrow differences trains the eye. Training the eye conditions the soul.

A Word about Loss

Conditioning the soul can be one of the functions of loss. But loss turned to unresolved grief, a possibility I am aware of in myself, can have crippling effects. I am thinking of a visit I had yesterday with my "refugee gardener" friend. She wanted me to meet a friend of hers, who was visiting, while temporarily unhoused. Portly, graying, and, I guessed, slightly older than my friend, the visitor was one of those who lost their homes in the great Oakland fire of 1991. As we sipped our herbal tea and nibbled at almond cookies, I learned that she lived on her own in recurring short-term rentals and house-sitting gigs and suffered from various ailments, including, from her general tone, what looked to me like depression.

Her grief over the loss of her house seemed to express itself in the whole posture of her body, the contours of which appeared to be sliding downward like a watercolor in the rain. A retired teacher, she had lost her house and all her papers, books, reports, and manuscripts, including a novel she had just been finishing. Everything she had burned to the ground. All her memories and hopes turned into ash. As she talked, describing her traumatic journey from the fire to the present, her trauma appeared live, as if it all had happened yesterday.

Her litany of places almost acquired and lost was one of flat resignation. Places were either way too expensive or otherwise not to her taste. Too near to the city or too far from it. Nothing she looked at was right. Nothing could replace what she had lost. Nothing could console her for the life that had gone up in smoke. My friend, from her own history of loss and displacement, and I, with my house on the market due to circumstances of our own making, were both understanding and supportive, but after the visitor left, Sophie said, in a low voice as if the woman already down the road could hear, "Her real tragedy is that she can't let go."

Walking home after the visit, I felt an uncomfortable resonance, as if I'd been identifying with the woman's loss. And that felt suddenly wrong. Our circumstances are in no way like hers, I reminded myself. She's suffering a natural disaster and life-shattering loss. We are not like that. We are not "losing" anything. Our disaster, if it comes to that, is of our own making. We are experiencing the consequence of our own decisions. I saw this, in a moment of clarity, as if someone had pulled back the curtains in a dank and moldy room and let in the light. Our circumstances were not hers. Like many others in this volatile economic time, we were riding the times we were in on the willful steeds of our own desires. How we managed was up to fate and to us.

That this thought came as a surprise took me aback. I thought I'd already learned this. But wisdom—learning to live—is not like learning to ride a bike, where you learn it and never forget it and that's that. Learning to live is more like growing a garden—things are constantly sprouting, fading, dying, blooming, getting fungus, being eaten by white flies, changing, renewing, surprising you, disappointing you, delighting you, and even plunging you into moments of rapture. Or despair. All that.

Weather, too, has its fickleness. You just never know. And that is how I am now. Continually experiencing moments of insight, continually forgetting, then remembering, and forgetting again. Continually hoping to learn, really learn, how to be—how to see, how to love, and how to cope when everything changes all over again in a moment, or series of moments, of surprise.

Night of the Broken Crockery

Gray. Clouds fisting up. The morning is poised to explode in rain. A welcome relief after last night's emotional storm. I'm standing barefoot on the cold floorboards in the silent kitchen, grinding the coffee beans. At first glance nothing has changed. But when I reach for my favorite cup, it is gone. Oh. Right. I look around the room. The open shelves that hold my best dishes, the lovely hand-painted Italian cups and bowls I'd brought from my home back east, were oddly sparse. Ping of sadness. I reach for a lesser mug that happened to survive, pour my coffee into the filter, let it drip, pull on a jacket, take the mug, smelling the comforting, aromatic steam, and step out onto the deck.

The big blue bird on the roof of the house squawks once when I appear. The scrub jay. He has beauty and initiative and absolute self-confidence, but when it came to giving out the voice talent, the gods must have been out on a break. While all the other little nondescript birds twitter and sing with delicate musicality, this handsome guy just goes *Squawk!* But there is a pattern to his squawking. As I head toward my little Casita, my place of peace and solitude, he swoops down to the tip of the apple tree beside my deck and waits. He does this every day. This is a habit we have formed. He wants some birdseed. I want to tame him.

Squawk! he calls, like the sound of a rusty hinge. *Squawk!*

"I'm coming!"

He bobs his head and waits while I reach the Casita, get the seed from the pail I keep on the step, and approach the feeder. I pour some seed in my hand and hold it out to the bird.

Now I say, *"Come down here!"*

He does not.

No? No. I pour the seed in the little feeder dish and back away a few steps.

How about this close? Still, no. He watches and ruffles his beautiful wings.

Squawk!

I step up to the deck and stand by the door. Now?

Now! He spreads his wings and makes a graceful arc, like a blue-drenched paint brush onto a canvas, down to the feeder.

Ah. We are relating. This is so much easier than what happens up in the house with my beloved. These days, with the air between us heavy with unspoken accusations and fears, the simplest effort at communication can end up in a row. One verbal misstep leads to a correction, and that launches an explanation, and that triggers an accusation, and then the whole thing spirals upward, and, if we're not able to disengage, explodes in the slamming of doors. It's like the proverbial briar patch. The harder we try to get out of it, whatever it is, the more intractable it all gets. By the end, I don't even know what we're arguing about.

Yesterday was one of those days. The real estate man called to show the house again. A nice couple. Interested. Definitely, interested. He was sure they'd be making an offer. Yadda, yadda. Could we straighten up and be gone by two o'clock? Yes, sure.

I hate them so much.

We got out of the house on time and drove over the hill, together, in silence. It was a misty afternoon. The coastal road through the majestic redwood forest was quintessential California. The glimpses of the ocean, shining and peaceful, reminded us, without our having to say it, how much we loved this place—and did not want to leave. We drove up Mount Tamalpais, the local, sacred mountain, and found a favorite scenic pull over and stopped. All the Pacific Ocean seemed to spread out in front of us. All this land, all this possibility and hope. Sitting in the car, listening to the mystical Celtic tones of Enya, windows down to let in the spicy air, I thought, but did not say, *How stupid of us if we can't make this life work!* Not that I blamed him or that he blamed me. Really. We each, deep down, blamed ourselves, and that was worse. So, we said nothing. Enya, in her maddening serenity, crooned on.

Driving back through streets full of restaurants, we realized we were hungry. Famished. We hadn't had time for lunch, and now it was getting dark, dinner time, and a long way back. But in the mood we were in, we couldn't decide whether to starve or spend money we didn't have. There was no right choice.

"We could get some Chinese," I said, in what I hoped was a helpful voice.

"That costs money we don't have," he said.

"Everything costs money we don't have!" I said, very consciously not adding, *Why else would we be selling the house!*

"Are you that hungry?"

"I guess not."

"But you want to go to a restaurant!"

"No. No. Not really."

"But it's what you want!"

"Only if you do!"

"There you go again!" He explodes.

"Oh, no. Don't start!" I beg.

"You're the one who said you wanted to eat!" He was yelling now.

"But I said I don't care!" I was yelling back.

So stupid. All of it.

Suddenly, he lurched the car over into a parking space. Across the street was Jenny Lowe's Chinese Restaurant, our favorite when we were flush. He was still yelling at me even as he switched off the car, slammed the door, and stormed across the street. I slunk down into my seat wondering why all this was happening and how it would end.

Almost immediately, there was a tapping on my window.

"Ma'am?" a young cop leaned his face in as I rolled the window down. "Ma'am, are you all right?" He had soft brown eyes and straight dark hair and such a young, sweet face.

"Yes. Thanks, officer," I said.

"He looked pretty angry."

"He's just a little upset."

"He looked a lot upset to me," he said, looking over at the retreating figure, then into the car, casting his eyes into the back seat, then driver's side, then back into my eyes, the way he would if he had a flashlight. I assured him that my husband was kind and good and that I was in no danger.

"You know," he said carefully, "domestic violence, abuse, it's not just hitting." He paused as if he hated having to say this out load. "It's yelling, causing a disturbance, making you afraid." He reached into his pocket and pulled out a card and handed it to me. "Call these people if you ever feel afraid. They're here to help." He then said good night and told me to remember to call if I ever needed help.

I looked at the card and a shiver went down my spine. Abused Women's Support Services. *Abused?* Me? I was loved, not abused. I'd never been abused. Had I? But these rows were distressing and were getting worse. They were almost becoming a habitual blast of reaction to every little thing, while the lumbering big thing—our future—shambled on, lethal and intolerable underneath a cloud of silence, making us both miserable.

When he got back into the car and handed me the bag of lovely smelling Chinese food, I told Robert about the cop, and he looked mortified. He sat silent a minute. I put the bag on the floor by my feet. Then he held out his hand. I took it. Said nothing more.

By the time we got home, it was dark. As we pulled into the drive alongside the house, the headlights struck a white form. Lily! Tail high, pacing back and forth, the cat was telling us, in every way available to her species, that something was badly amiss. I looked at my husband.

"What's she doing out?" We never leave her out. She's a city cat. There are foxes.

"I thought you put her in."

"I did." Would the real estate man have let her out? Surely not. I made a move and Lily turned and tiptoed, tail high, towards the door. I followed. Then I saw it.

"Oh, my God," I said, "there's been an earthquake!" The sliding glass door was open a couple of inches. Inside, the shining pine floor was covered with broken crockery, vases, glasses, my lovely hand-painted Italian dishes—cups, bowls, plates, everything. These seem to have been flung from the open shelves. Nothing in the closed cupboard was disturbed. Odd. Was it really an earthquake?

Stepping in, we looked around stupidly. What in the world? Then I heard a noise, coming from the bedroom. I rushed down the three steps into the room and there, half rising on her haunches in innocent, nearsighted befuddlement, was a small raccoon. I recognized her as one of the evening regulars on our deck, her front paws under her chin, fingering each other in anxiousness.

"Little One? Baby? Baby! Is it you?"

Baby, black beady little bandit eyes stared up at me. I was about to laugh, but at that instant, my husband, the great white Englishman for whom wildlife had no place in a proper human abode, rushed in, pushing me out of the way.

"Stop!" he cried. "Be careful! He might be rabid!"

Rabid? Baby?

"Careful!" He repeated and grabbed a straight-backed chair and thrust it, lion tamer style, at the little creature. Unable to watch without laughing, I left him, all 6'3" of him, bellowing at the raccoon while I went on to survey the damage in the front room. Oh, my wedding vase from Carol! Oh, the ugly-charming big vase Robert and I bought at a fair in town one day when we were not speaking, but, seeing this thing, laughed and made up. Everything, everything broken in shatters all over the hard pine floor. So many little moments of civility, remnants of my eastern, sophisticated life, lost. Crazy. Why do we live here? Maybe my mother was right. This whole California thing was nuts. On that note, I realized that my husband was bellowing for me.

I hurried back to the bedroom. Baby had climbed up the drapes and was cowering, chirring down at him as he still threatened her with the chair. I sighed, walked past the great him, opened the bedroom's sliding glass door, and stepped back to let Baby scramble down from the drapes and waddle past me out the door. "Bad Baby," I said, uselessly. "Go on. Out!" My great English raccoon tamer joined me at the door, and we watched while the little creature slunk, shamed, out the door and across the deck. Sad. We liked Baby. Well, not so much right then.

A survey of the house indicated that it had been an extraordinary evening. Every shelf on the kitchen walls had things overturned, broken, or spilled. Plants in pots by the door were plundered. The trail of destruction led from the kitchen to the dining room to the bedroom, and even into the bathroom—where the trail was not merely horizontal, but vertical as well, with little muddy raccoon footprints at the ceiling of the tiled shower stall. What on earth? Back in the kitchen, we saw that the cat food bag had not been ransacked, so food had not been the motive. So what was this? A raccoon rave? Did all the furry family take off at the sound of our approaching car, leaving Baby alone to take the blame?

We pondered the evidence. We stared at Lily for clues. We examined the doors again. No reasonable answer presented itself other than that the real estate man had left a door open. But he wouldn't have. We were baffled. Did the raccoons actually open the door themselves—they're famous for their burglary skills—and find Lily inside, and then all eight of them and the cat took off in a crazy chase? Did the raccoons and cat conspire to act out the energy of our own buried, unspeakable frustration?

We were also seriously hungry. Robert went out to the car to get the forgotten Chinese food. I cleared off the table by the window and wiped it down with disinfectant. A strange act, cleaning raccoon footprints from the dining room table. I washed a couple of remaining plates and put them on the table. It didn't seem right to sit at the table and eat without first cleaning and tidying the whole place, but in a way, it seemed fitting to just dine amidst the rubble, which was all somehow our fault.

We both knew that, in some way, whatever was happening—break it all, lose it all—we were responsible. We chose our path and here is where it led us. In Jungian psychology, we might call this raccoon invasion a moment of synchronicity. Two completely unrelated events—our argument, complete with the policeman's intervention, and the raccoon jamboree—seemed to coalesce into one neon-screaming lesson about the nature of this moment in time. Everything about to be broken. I wanted to cry.

But then my tired husband clomped up the steps and slid open the door. Poor him. His face looked ravaged. When he saw the table cleared for the food, he smiled. "Surprise," he said, holding out the great white bag. "It's still hot. Let's eat now and clean up after dinner!" I pushed away some dishes and went to him and hugged him.

Chinese had never tasted so good.

New Moon, New Men

Frogs. It is 7 p.m. and the frogs are singing—If you can call it singing—that orgiastic screaming that rises from the swale and makes me want to run down dark lanes, roll in grass, grab anyone handy, and dance. A sound that brings the shadows to life. What are the frogs so thrilled about? Is it something about the sky? Tonight's new moon? I know so little about the sky. Every night it covers me up with its blanket of stars, and I feel secure in the majesty of its expanse. Will the sky be different where I am going? And where is that? No. Don't try to answer, all that is somewhere in the fog-bound future. I must focus on the here and now.

Tonight my Ansel Adams calendar says that the new moon is in Pisces—my husband's moon. A sign of new beginnings. Thanks to the card the young cop gave me that night in Mill Valley, he has found a local men's group dedicated to stopping what they call men's violence against women.

The group leader, I'll call him Pete, a tall, thin, soft-spoken man who wears jeans and a sweatshirt and walks softly in Nikes, is, as Robert described him after the first meeting, a pure force of love. He welcomes all the men in his group with understanding and compassion—whether they're nice men like my husband, sent by their "end-of-their-rope" wives, or surly, knuckle-bruised felons, sent to the group by the courts. Men come to this group from all walks of life, in all ages, shapes, and colors. They bond with each other on the level of what they come to see as their essential life struggle—dealing with the out-of-control force that each one of them learns to refer to as "my violence."

From the moment he made the call, the first challenge for Robert was the word itself: *violence*, as in violence against women. And its sidekick: *abuse*, as in verbal and emotional abuse or abuse against women. Such words were never used by nice men whose mothers taught them early that you never hit a girl. Words like *violence* or *abuse* were not part of their male self-image. Robert said as much to Pete, that first night, in front of the group. Sure, he'd said, he needed some help with communication and maybe some work on his temper, but he wasn't a violent man. "I'm not that sort of person!" Robert told me with a wry smile, adding that Pete had smiled, and an audible smirk had rippled through the group. "Right," Pete said, "you're not that sort. Neither are most of these guys. But they're all violent. Like you. Take a seat."

I read with an amazement of recognition, an inner shower of relief the literature Robert brought home. *They understand!* I thought. The core principle of the group, the one unmodifiable standard that every man in the group must accept is that violence against women is never excusable. No matter what "she did," how much "she asked for it," how much "she deserved it," whether "she made me do it," or any of the other howls and excuses that men can hurl at women, Pete's principle, inviolate rule was that there is no excuse ever for violence against a woman. A man must learn to manage the emotions within him that drive his violence.

Now comes the tricky bit: just what do they mean by violence? For the most part, for well brought up "nice" men like Robert, it's only in the movies that they see slapping, punching, and other physically abusive treatment of women, and they righteously hate it. But in Pete's "violent men's group," when the court-ordered bruisers tell their stories about how, in fits of rage, they almost (or had) knocked out or strangled their wives or partners, the other "nice" men feel a chill of recognition and say to themselves, "There, but for the grace of God..."

What all men have in common, as Robert related to me that he'd learned, is a culture-deep, inbred, age-old male control and domination mindset that, when feeling threatened, triggers a primitive instinct—to defend, to fight, to strike out. And this is supported by male cultural norms. "Pete learned and now shows us how to recognize the emotional triggers," he told me. "And how to recognize our moment of feeling threatened, when we feel what Pete calls our 'fatal peril.' This could be something as small as the moment when a discussion of whether to have oatmeal or eggs rockets up into a row. At that point, Pete taught the men to say to themselves, *This is my moment of fatal peril—I will not die.* And then to stop. Pause. Ask for time out to breathe, nurture themselves, and remind themselves that however panicked the woman has made them feel, they will not die. Not right then, at least. Here, in the pause, was a safe moment. A moment in which to take a time out and remember oneself." So now, in our arguments, my "violent man" is learning to say, *Time Out!* And I'm learning to stop, back off, let the dust settle, drop the victim mindset. He's not the enemy. I'm not to blame. Let him go to his room and collect himself. And for myself, do the same.

Like breaking any habit, this is not easy. Because "violence" is a reciprocal dynamic between the male and female, it's clear to me that men can't change without their women cooperating in the process of change. I met some of the men and their girlfriends and wives one evening at a local restaurant and was touched at how grateful the men were that finally, someone, Pete and other men, had shown them how to accept their feelings. One such man, whom Robert particularly liked, a former executive in a large, prestigious firm, wearing a car salesman's smile and an expensive sports jacket, introduced himself by way of his story.

"I lost my job because I was such an asshole," he said, standing at the buffet table with his arm around his glamorous, blonde, well-coiffed wife, Betsy. "I always had to know better than everyone and always had to have the last word. I was using all my power to control everybody else, and when I got home, I just took it all out on Betsy, until she told me it was time to get help or get out." Betsy, willowy and quiet, with the composure of someone used to pouring tea, gave his arm a little squeeze and met my eyes shyly. "It's so much better now. We're both learning," she said, smiling, though her eyes looked tired. "I don't know where it's going, but now we have hope."

When I caught Pete momentarily alone, for once not surrounded by his people, I asked him what I could do to support my husband and help to "deactivate" our arguments. He laughed and his eyes twinkled. "I like to ask the group, 'Who here wants to be happy?' And they all raise their hands. Then I ask, 'And who here wants to be right?' Again, they all raise their hands. Then I say, 'And if you can't have both?' Then they stare at the floor and shuffle their feet." He waits for me to get it, and laughs. "We all think being right will make us happy." He shakes his head, still smiling. "This is hard to unlearn." Unconscious as it is, the "male role belief system," as they call it, is at odds with female equality. Complicated. Challenging. No wonder men are scared. No wonder both partners are walking on eggshells.

I think about my father. My father is no stranger to arguments. My mother had to take herself and her career to New York to get some peace. Now, in his old age, in the infrequent times I see him, he was wise. Was it just age? Was living by himself all these years enough to convince him to work on himself? I don't know. But certain ingrained, culturally supported patterns like male dominance do not change on their own, and so I suspect he had some inspirational intervention along the way. Someday, maybe I'll ask him.

10

The Lack of Racoons

I haven't seen our little raccoon family for a few weeks. Shortly after the great "Baby Invasion," they started not showing up at the deck at dinnertime. First, Little One, then Mrs. Rocky and her two new babies. Even the year-old baby. No show. What was going on?

Neighbors said they noticed their raccoons disappearing too. There were rumors around of distemper. Maybe rabies. But how could our creatures be sick? We feed them Science Diet! Maybe, as my husband offered one weepy morning, the family just went off on a long journey. (I imagined them, arguing, Little One begging Mrs. Rocky not to make them go, Mrs. Rocky's mature insistence, their stuffing little backpacks with extra masks, maps, stashes of extra cat food, and then all of them waddling sadly down the dirt road to escape whatever plague it was we humans could not see. For as long as we have known them and after all we have done for them, wouldn't you think they'd have said goodbye?

Even now, still, every night I watch for them. But the deck beyond the glass doors stays empty. Sometimes I find myself pacing and wondering if there isn't someone I should be phoning, and I realize I've called everyone. Nobody's seen the raccoons. And I turn alone in the room, and I feel something I haven't felt since I've been on this land: a kind of grief, almost a loneliness.

Lonely? you say. For raccoons?

In a recent *Star Trek* rerun, which we like to watch while I make dinner, Data, the personable android, explained the phenomenon of friendship in terms of mutual familiarity with various electrical response patterns and frequency variations or something that, put another way, boils down to: I've grown accustomed to your face. Over the last few years, we have grown accustomed to a line of pointy, masked little faces at the sliding glass door—first one, then four, then eight, now five furry, bright creatures positioned for maximum cuteness, as if auditioning for Disney, sitting upright, spidery hands pressed to the glass, soft little bellies sagging schmoo-like, watching my every move, licking their lips, and beaming their one intention into me as I go about preparing dinner. I think of the petitioning nature of prayer. Do we look like that to the Divine?

Raccoons—this is little known, but true—are capable of transspecies friendship. Here is the proof: It happened a while ago, after I had returned from a week's trip east. It was 9:30 the morning. I had just gone to the front door with my coffee, and who should appear, but Little One. A raccoon for breakfast? Unheard of. These guys are nocturnal. But sure enough, bright sunlight and all, here she was. I got some food for her, put it down on the mat, and moved past her across the deck to sit on the step. She gobbled the food, maneuvering the bits with both hands, shoving them delicately into her mouth, and then she waddled over and sat near me. That's all. We just sat together for a while.

When I rose and went down the steps to the lower deck and leaned over to the railing to look out at the garden, she followed, and sat behind me. That's all. I looked down at her; she looked up at me. Little pointy face. Bright, beady eyes. She was not hungry. So, what? I said, "Little One, did you miss me?" She watched me, her beautiful silver fur shining in the soft morning glow, her ringed tail fluffy, her black eyes shining with intelligence. Just two years old, she looked so new, so fresh. A perfect creature. I felt that she wanted to tell me something, but I couldn't figure out what it was. Maybe, as I feel sometimes in a particular patch of light, she simply wanted to be in the presence of an energy larger than herself. Maybe there was trouble in raccoon world. Who could know? Then the sound of the sliding glass door pulling open. Robert laughing at something he'd just read in the news and wanted to tell me. Little One scampered under the house.

Raccoons—and this is another little-known fact—can be taught manners. Unlike their mother, Mrs. Rocky, who always reached for her piece of bread like a dowager reaching for a teacup, Little One and her siblings attacked the food like jackals. Twice, as my extended hand stayed too long in the fray, their razor-sharp teeth accidentally grazed my finger. I rinsed it immediately, though it hadn't drawn blood, a little sheepish over my caution. Rabies? Nah, look at them, I thought, healthy as I am. No need to worry. Nevertheless, realizing that such bad manners could make for dangerous adults, I decided to train them.

To train a raccoon, you must anticipate their movements with accurate timing and precise aim and engage the principle of reward and repetition, as you would in any training process. Here is how you do it: You get comfortable in the doorway, sit way low, then sloooowly hold out a nice piece of bread, watch their eyes, or any slight ripple on the fur on their shoulders, and as they get ready to dive for it, snatch away your hand. My husband was braver at this than I. He would let them climb up onto his lap. But neither of us was so reckless as to try to pet them.

As you pull away the bread, the fat little babies will sit back and frown at you and lick their lips and wonder what's up. Don't be fooled. They are not chastised, they are watching for any twitch in your hand, so they can pounce before you pull it back. The tension mounts. Now! They dive. Now! You jerk your hand back. If all goes well, they'll land just short of the bread and then decide whether to reach out with their little hands. Ah, there. Do this a couple of times and they will learn to take the bread slowly and carefully with their hands, not their teeth, which might miss and get your finger instead. This avoidance of injury and resulting consequence, to a human translates as "politeness." It is the essence of manners.

During my "training" sessions, I became aware of a familiar social dynamic: Threat of insufficiency overrides civility. As with humans, this trait is first perpetrated upon strangers. Once, we watched a little fox tiptoe up to the deck as all eight raccoons were hunkered down to their dinner. Their thick silver fur rippled on their backs as their hands, sensitive as those of the blind, felt around for food and fingered it into their pointy little maws, which worked up and down like scissors or the way children mouth a bite too hot for the tongue. Totally given over to feasting, the deck was alive with the sounds of crunching. The hungry fox sneaked up to the unoccupied end of the pile and snatched a bite, then retreated to the shadows to gulp it down. He did this again and again, with only the barest notice on the part of the raccoons. Very nice.

However, as the pile went down, the dynamic shifted. The raccoons, seeing an end to the meal, suddenly acknowledged the stranger in their midst and snarled, driving him off the deck. Then, the foreign threat dispatched but with diminished food to share, they went after each other, and the orderly line of diners broke into balls of slavering greed. We found this very funny and assumed that raccoons, much like humans, do not burden themselves with selfless generosity and just do what they do, and that was fun to watch—until the night we went into town and came home late.

Now, they're all gone, gone with all the answers we'll never know, and worse, with no farewell.

I am thinking these things as I stand at the kitchen island, making my coffee. I take a cup in to my husband in the bedroom, put it on his bedside table, and tiptoe away. Then I pull open the glass door, walk out onto the cool deck and stand, for a moment, outside. Soft, rising sun is glowing over the eucalyptus, through the mist. I wonder if Little One had been, in her raccoon way, trying to tell me something. My imagination wanders, into the mist, and into the world of raccoons.

Mrs. Rocky's Tale

It was the tail end of what Northern California considers winter. The days were short, the nights were chilly, and the rains were almost done. A good time of year for raccoons. The dense brambles of the Blackberry Sea that housed Mrs. Rocky's network of tunnels kept her family nest dry and warm.

But lately, Mrs. Rocky was preoccupied. She hardly ate. Each night, she led her family to the deck, grabbed a few bites from the cat dish, politely took a piece of bread from one of the humans' hands, then scuttled back into the shadows to chew and pace, leaving Little One and Baby and the two other younger ones crunching and quarreling while the humans, sitting by the glass door, smiled and watched. All seemed normal, but something was wrong. Mrs. Rocky could feel it, like a storm cloud hovering, not yet overhead, but moving closer, like a great, slavering, invisible dog.

Mrs. Rocky tried to believe that her fears were unreal. Life here was good. She loved her nest and all her babies and had a certain affection for her humans who lived in the big house just up the path from the Blackberry Sea. She remembered knocking on the door of the big house that first summer. The humans, a female and her mate, seemed to be new to the place and welcomed her with pieces of bread, a nice bucket of water, and little piles of crunchy food. This was most convenient as Mrs. Rocky had new babies at the time, and the less foraging she had to do, the better. When her babies were old enough, she brought them to the deck with her two older ones. The female human laughed at them, "They look like little soup cans!" Her mate, a tall, blonde male, made funny contraptions with sticks and bones and rubber bands, which he dangled in front of the round, little babies who grabbed at the objects, just to humor him. He meant well, but really, what did he think they were, cats?

Speaking of cats. The humans called her Lily. Pure white, haughty, and vain, she reacted to raccoons as anyone would to a terrible smell—tiptoeing wide around them, hairs raised, hissing, as they rudely crunched and fingered their food into their mouths. When Lily happened to be inside and the raccoon family appeared at the door, she would fling herself at the glass, growling and spitting. "Knock yourself out," they thought, and pleasantly settled into their meal. A cat is no match for a raccoon.

Sometimes the humans, who seemed to have no babies of their own and very little to do, just sat on the floor by the door and watched as the "Rockies" scooped the crunchy bits into their mouths. Mrs. Rocky noticed that they sat close together, with their arms around each other, appearing to be comforting each other, much the way she and Little One often sat with their arms around their babies.

Mrs. Rocky was very careful to take the bread the humans offered gently with her delicate, monkey-like hands, so as not to scare them. The babies, however, snatched the offered bits in their jaws, frightening the humans, who jerked back their hands and cried, "No, no! Bad babies!" then laughed when the babies scrambled away and peeked back at them from under the chaise. The humans couldn't tell that the babies were laughing too.

Humans were easily trained. After three years, Mrs. Rocky had them feeding her out of their hands. She taught the babies that if they should take on certain poses—sitting up on their hind legs, lounging on their elbows, draping themselves over flowerpots, or pressing on the glass with their two little hands or nose—the humans would smile and come right out with another handful of food. If all those tricks failed, Little One could stare at the female human very, very intensely while licking her pointy lips. The female human would rush right out with treats. Worked every time.

Once their little bellies were filled, the Rockies would waddle off the deck and down to the path and through the hole and into the tunnels that led to their warm, dry nest where they all giggled and curled up and slept. Life was good.

Until now.

It was a Friday night, and a bright moon was climbing up over the scratchy cypress tops on the east horizon. Mrs. Rocky called the babies to her in their meeting place under the house to say that what she dreaded most in the world was at hand.

"Little One, babies," she said, "Listen carefully. The time has come that we must leave our home and go far away."

The little group looked up and blinked and could not believe their ears. "But why?" they in fearful chirring voices, their beady black eyes wide with shock, their pointy little jaws working soundlessly, and their delicate hands pulling at their silvery fur. "Why would we want to leave our home?"

"Because," Mrs. Rocky said, very solemnly, "If we stay, we are all going to die."

There was a gaping silence, like the moment before an earthquake, and then they all cried and wailed, and Baby, who was still not quite grown up, wailed loudest of all.

"No! Why? This can't be happening to us!"

Mrs. Rocky tried to be patient, but there was urgency in her voice: "There is a plague in the land," she explained. "Many raccoons in the town and our neighboring woods have sickened and died already. Even the foxes are dying. If we are to survive, we need to leave."

Now everyone was crying. To leave their home was unthinkable. Here, on this lovely acre surrounded by brambles and woods, they had everything baby raccoons could want: a protective Blackberry Sea with miles of tunnels all to themselves, soft clearings of grass where they could sit on late summer afternoons and bat at thistle pods and watch the silky plumes sail into the sun. Here, in the fall, when they were tired of eating blackberries, there were enough apple trees in the garden to keep them delirious and fat. And best of all, was the friendly deck, with flower planters to lounge in, the water bucket to splash in, a nice lounge chair, silly cat, and tame humans to see to their every need. It was heaven. And, for the babies at least, it was all they had ever known.

"I'm not leaving, and you can't make me!" said Baby.

"But how can we leave our humans?" said Little One. "What will we do without them?"

"There will be other humans."

"But these are our humans! We've known them all our lives!" The others joined in. "No, no! They'll miss us!"

Mrs. Rocky sighed. This would be more difficult than she thought.

The night was very still. They could hear the frogs screaming in the nearby lagoon. They could hear the bamboo rustling gently outside the entrance to their meeting place under the house. They were all, even Mrs. Rocky, afraid. The babies were afraid because they were going out into the dreadful unknown. Mrs. Rocky was afraid it might already be too late.

"Are you really, really, really sure?" asked Baby in a tiny voice.

Mrs. Rocky thought about the news of the plague she'd been hearing, turned to Little One, and said, "Remember the time the big dog attacked our burrow and bit off the end of your tail?" How could Baby forget? They'd been about to cross the meadow to the deck for supper when this black, slavering beast appeared, towering over them. All the raccoons dove into the brush, but having been first out, Baby was last in, and as she dove for the hole, something clamped down onto her tail. Her world turned white with pain. She struggled free and it was only after she reached the nest that she realized that her beautiful tail had been shortened by several rings.

"Remember how brave you were," her mother continued, "even though you cried and cried?"

"Yes," she sniffed.

"Remember how you said you'd never let a vicious old dog catch you again?"

"Yes," she sniffed.

"Well," whispered Mrs. Rocky while all the others strained to hear, "What is after us is like that vicious dog, except that it is invisible, and it is so vicious that if it gets close to us, it will devour us all."

At that point, Little Bear, the smallest one, began to cry, and it was all Mrs. Rocky could do to keep from sobbing herself. "Little Bear," she said, nuzzling the furry little baby raccoon, "you must have courage. We are leaving to save our lives."

Mrs. Rocky looked up at the sky. The moon was high now, casting a milk-white light on all the contours of the land, illuminating the path leading from the house through the meadow to the main entrance to their burrows in the Blackberry Sea. The five raccoons filed out of the meeting place under the house and waddled down the path to their burrows to pack for their trip.

Mrs. Rocky stuffed into five little packs all the essentials the raccoon family would need for their journey: extra masks, little safe-cracking kits for refrigerators and garbage bins, tiny crowbars for cupboards and drawers, can openers, nail files, maps, and charts.

While Mrs. Rocky packed, Little One did what she usually did in times of stress: she lay back on her elbow and pulled at her silvery hairs, gazing about in prayerful detachment. "This is not happening," she thought. "Let's just go up to the deck and get a nice meal and wake up from this terrible dream. Plague. Huh! My mother is so negative."

Mrs. Rocky threw at her a verbal rock. "Little One! Wake up! Or the Invisible Dog will get us!" Little One scrambled, blinking, to her feet. Truly, she'd never had to do much in her whole young life at all. She'd spent her days sleeping and her evenings draped over flowerpots, eating when she felt like it, and lounging on the deck like a pelt. Now she would have to grow up—and fast.

When they were all assembled and ready to go, the two youngsters plus Baby and Little One lined up, hats on, packs filled, sniffing and blinking with excitement and sorrow and fear. They were leaving their home for good. It was time to say goodbye.

Raccoons, like all wild things, bid goodbye in great stillness and with intense concentration. *Goodbye*, they said in their raccoon way, to the hidden garden down by the little house with the birdbath, which Little One still couldn't reach. *Goodbye* to the bamboo, which rustled so nicely in the wind. *Goodbye* to the little plum tree, which the big blue bird practically bent over when it landed in it, and, deep in the Blackberry Sea, *goodbye* to the hidden entrance hole to their tunnel network. *Goodbye*, they said, to the place underneath the little building where the female human spent her days, and where, in the summer afternoons, they would gather and wait till she set out for the house and then scramble after her up the hill for dinner.

Finally, and this was hardest of all, *goodbye* big house. Their humans' house, their own meeting place underneath, their deck, their humans. How could they explain their leaving to their humans?

As they stood on the path in a tight little bunch, beaming their goodbyes, Lily, the cat, appeared. They all looked at each other. Could they ask the cat to explain to the humans? The cat was smarter than the humans, for sure, but that still didn't make her a genius. How could they explain to her about the plague?

Lily watched them and they watched her. Slowly, she began to understand. The hairs on her back relaxed, and she sat down, wrapped her silky, white tail around her prim front paws and listened. They all stared at each other, the raccoons beaming to the cat: *Tell them it's like an invisible dog, that's coming to kill us. Tell them we said good-bye.* And the cat beamed to the raccoons, *I'll try, but it's hard to make humans understand; they think everything is about them.*

Then all the raccoons went up to the deck one last time, nosed around, scooped up any last bits of food, turned over their dish, put some new handprints on the glass door, nodded to the cat, and then scuttled down the steps with heavy hearts. They were ready to go.

At the bottom of the steps, Mrs. Rocky sat back and sighed. She was feeling terribly tired, and she felt the danger stiffening the fur on her neck. It was time to go. The invisible dog was near, she could feel it. There was a chill creeping through her, and she didn't want the others to see. She wiped her nose. There was only one thing to be done.

"Little One," she said. "I want you to go now and lead the way. Take Baby and the others, go to the road, and turn toward the sound of the big roar. When you get to the edge of the land, look up. See that brightest star?" She pointed to the North Star, burning brightly overhead. "Follow that. I will stay behind to secure our tunnels. I'll catch up in a day or two."

"What? Me?" Little One was shocked out of her sadness. "I can't go off by myself. I can't take care of all these babies. I don't know anything about stars. I've never been away from home! I'm hungry!" Little One was frightened. She simply didn't know if she could cope.

Mrs. Rocky lunged at her. "Go!" she snarled. "And babies, you follow Little One. Obey her as if she were me. Hurry now. Go!"

Little One backed away from her mother, looking one last time over the moonlit acre that had been her home. There was life beyond this acre, she could hear it. And there was light if she could just follow the moon. Yes. Out there in the dark lay waiting all the unknown things she would learn about. She would go toward them bravely but would never forget this place, her humans, her home. With that, she turned abruptly and struck out down the milk-white lane, head low, back hunched, her silvery fur rippling in the moonlight. Baby and the two round little ones with their caps and back packs scurried after her.

Mrs. Rocky watched until the last shadow had disappeared into the night. When all was quiet, she sat up and wiped her eyes with her spidery hands, then studied her palms for any signs of the plague. Then, licking her palms, she lowered herself and disappeared into the bushes.

Goodbye Eyes

It's many days since I sat with Little One out on the deck. Now the deck is desperately still. No bright little eyes peer in the window. No pointy little face peeks out from the flowerpot, or from behind the bucket, or from under the chaise. No little hands or black nose press against the glass. No little bearlike form sits upright at the door, licking her lips and telepathically commanding, *Food! Right here! Me! Me!* And no languid character lounges on the chaise.

We both are thinking that somewhere out there, Mrs. Rocky and Little One and Baby and the youngsters are all safe and snug in some distant new home, happy together in the goodness of life, tucked in underneath this magnificent blanket of stars.

Meanwhile, this time the buyer seems really serious. She has gathered a few friends together to make the down payment. She's single, but will share the place with her boyfriend, so she says. They are both in their fifties and, therefore, stable, or so it would seem, the real estate man assured us. Financing would be tricky, but it's always tricky, and they were offering full price. So we could find no real reason to refuse.

At the same time, our desperation to sell has been fading lately as various contracts have fallen through. Meanwhile, each of us has been casting out for freelance work to bring in needed funds. He's been doing some consulting. I've been putting my camera to work. So we are, in a sense, evening out the field, allowing for acceptance of what happens, getting ready for what we dread, hoping for whatever is best.

Nevertheless, ready for anything, I am seeing my world through "goodbye eyes." Goodbye, Yardbirds Hardware Store, where we shopped together for the plants for my first California garden. Pansies, sweet alyssum, petunias. I planted them all in neat, color-coordinated rows, just like my garden at home. I was pleased with myself until my friend and former landlady, said, when she stopped by to see if I had time for a walk, "It looks like Versailles!" This was not a compliment. "We like native plants here," she said. Right. But not to worry. Nature went ahead and erased my gaffe. Slugs. Deer. What didn't get them from above got them from below.

So, goodbye, Rafael Lumber, the lumber yard of dreams, where we bonded as new homeowners, laughing and arguing down the wide aisles, buying tools and supplies for our modest renovation, feeling the world open to endless possibility.

Our optimism made some people nervous. At a "welcome to your new home" dinner at a neighbor's house, we admired the work they were doing on their kitchen. Our hostess laughed. "Our architect told us he'd never seen a marriage survive a renovation." *Ha ha ha.* Her husband grinned. The other couples, all with sawdust on their own floors, shuffled and flashed toothy grins too. Anybody uncomfortable? More wine was poured, and we sat, chatting optimistically, not mentioning their unfinished living room. The host of that dinner is still working on the kitchen. His wife is now living with their architect, in Bali, in a place near the ocean where renovation is done by storms. We remind ourselves frequently how we got through our minor renovation when we moved in, marriage intact. So far.

This past Sunday evening, all dressed up, I headed out over the hill toward the city for a photography gathering at a friend's house in Mill Valley. Clear light. That golden glow. Smooth, white waves curling down below. Just as the coast road makes a turn into the redwood forest, I overtook a blue pickup truck with a sticker on the back saying, Women Should Be on Horses. Why not? Thirty seconds later, just after a hairpin curve with a precipitous cliff falling away hundreds of feet to the ocean, a wild vibration set up in my right front tire. Fear—physical, emotional, existential—surged through me. I was alone on a dangerous mountain road, my right front tire was flat, my credit cards were all at the max, and cell phones weren't yet ubiquitous. And I was in my best shoes.

I floppled around three hairpin corners to a pullout, grabbed my purse, jumped out of the car, locked the doors, and flagged down the pickup I'd just passed. Whew. That was easy. The nice woman—tanned, Levi jacket, long gray-blond hair in one fat braid down her back, was heading to Mill Valley, too, and was happy to ferry me over the mountain to a phone. We exchanged the expected small talk: "Oh, isn't this the most wonderful place in the world to live?" she said. "Oh, yes, it certainly is," I said. "Why would anyone want to live anywhere else?" she said. "I can't imagine," I said. "Just look at the mountain, look at the sea, you'll never find all this anywhere else," she said. "Oh, certainly not," I said. "Where do you live?" she asked. I live ... I live ...

By the time I got out of the truck at Whole Foods, I could have shot her without remorse. I found a pay phone, called my hero, who jumped in the car, drove over the mountain, and forty-five minutes later, with the usual cursing and banging, the tire was changed. He looked so handsome and wracked and flustered, worrying about what could have happened to me, that I blew off the meeting, and he and I went to dinner at Joe's Taco Lounge, where we laughed and ate tacos and did not discuss tires or money or real estate. It was bad, of course, the tire. And dangerous. And painful to have to be reminded all the time about our circumstance.

"See? It's all worked out," he said. "How's the corn cake?"

To me, starry-eyed optimists always sound fake. But I have to say, once a tire is changed, a positive attitude does make a better dinner companion. So much of our experience, I reminded myself again, is in how you choose to see it.

The Wedding Photographer

Out of all the photographers in the phone books of San Francisco and New York, she chose me. And I'm not even a wedding photographer. My spirit was developed in the aesthetically lofty darkrooms of Fine Art to deplore the genre. But, when an exclusive San Francisco event planner who was at wits' end to please a Bride who had rejected every photographer she'd shown her, came across my portfolio, the Bride screamed for joy. My "style" was just what she had in mind. The photographs—moody large format black and white scenes of people in woods, on cliffs, with cows, in fields, by streams—my "style" was just what this Bride had in mind.

    Except, she said, when she called me from New York, she didn't care so much for the woods or fields, just the faces, please. And some color. And, though she didn't want to be vain about it, "If I don't get at least one good picture of myself after all I've gone through, I will die."

    "No problem," I said, remembering a wedding of my own, in my former life, to a National Geographic photographer, before an assembly of National Geographic photographers, all armed and loaded for cover shots. But after hours of blazing Nikons, the only photo we ended up with was a snapshot taken with a One-Step by someone from the editorial staff. What happened to the pros? Was the challenge of happiness too much for them? Was it an omen, foretelling the ultimate dissolution of the match? Possibly. At any rate, aware as I was of the short and long-term potential for disaster in the wedding photography realm, how could I—a person most comfortable with inanimate things, rocks, roots, and people told to "freeze"—have signed up for a challenge upon which someone's very life depended? Well, desperate people do strange things. Rob banks. Kidnap babies. Take crack. Jump off the Golden Gate Bridge. I'd considered various options myself, experiencing a long stretch of one of those professional lulls through which fate loves to strengthen us. But, to get real, none of those options compared, in fright, drama, and possible dire consequence, to become, overnight, a wedding photographer.

Now, let us note, there are weddings, and there are Weddings. This wedding would be on the far end of Weddings. Two hundred-fifty some people, from England, Cambodia, Japan, New York, Aspen, Monterey, and who-knows-where, would descend on San Francisco in gala regalia to see The Bride, the statuesque brunette (whose aesthetic genius was lofty enough to recognize mine) and The Groom, a handsome English descendant of a lord. How would this turn out?

"Picture *Four Weddings and a Funeral*," said my husband, himself a subject of Her Majesty, and thankfully, not a photographer, Geographic or otherwise. Visual memory of the film called up something about hats, while visceral memory hovered uneasily around the "funeral" part. But there, the association ended: my artistic mind was intrigued by this bride. She was so New York. She hated everything. She terrified the gentle San Francisco event planners. Hated their florists, hated all their photographers, hated their fun ideas (a tugboat ride? Are you kidding?) Instead of arrangements of mums and gardenias, she favored lilies and wild grasses. Instead of bridesmaids in a row, dressed alike, she wanted an array of uniquely coifed and vested women fluttering about the church. Along with the "Ave Maria," she would have the organist play "Jerusalem." And to top it off, she told me, "I'll have a bagpiper in a kilt! Don't you love it?" Would I do it? I thought about my debts, set my fee at the highest end and—became, well, let's call it her Wedding Documentarian.

After the happiness of the (sizable and lifesaving) advance check, the project bubbled away in my anxiety zones, until I marshaled my forces, engaged all my past professionalism and began planning and drilling to master the eventualities, both expected and unexpected, of The Day. I was supported by solid professional habit and also fired up by a thin band of terror, rising at times to stark, staring disbelief: What am I doing? I'm not a wedding photographer! I don't even know how to work an on-camera flash! Instead of sleep, the nightmare of social and photographic catastrophe swam before me. By day, I went over and over coming events in my mind and on my white board.

First, and most favorite part of the event on the list, which I'd sold to the bride, was the Portrait Room. I had, in a moment of creative delirium, promised her a room set up in the Nob Hill mansion where the reception would take place, as a studio, so that all the guests could come, in couples, in groups, in whatever, in their finery, and have their fashion portraits made.

"Oh, I hope it won't be like Olan Mills," she said. "My dear," I said, "do not think Olan Mills. Think Avedon." (Forgive me, Mr. Avedon, and any true photographers. I really did say this. Such was my hubris!) Still, I could see the pictures. I loved them already. Problem was, I had no studio. Had never done such portraits. I'm an "environmental photographer." My lighting's done by God. In this mansion, there would be no chasing the magic light, no "waiting for the moment." I'd have to create the moment, and the magic, and hope that the person who walked into it would shine. I'd have to make it all happen.

Okay. Put that on the list.

Less easy to see in advance than the fashion portraits, were the "preparation pictures," the ones of the statuesque beauty and her attendants assembling the gossamer illusion that would become The Bride. The kind of pictures you see in Martha Stewart's wedding books. Which I'd ordered, to study. I could see the pictures, but to create sufficient magic, flattering light without God, I'd need... And here I had a brilliant stroke. An assistant schooled in wedding photography! I drew on my professional photographer contacts and, lo! Enter Jonathan, a cheerful fellow who loved his Vivitar strobe as much as I despise it. Lighting by Jonathan? A viable Plan B. Will do. But not quite right. Plan A would come to me.

Putting that part aside, I went on to the real killer: the Church. The march down the aisle. I have always pitied the wedding photographer, scurrying up the aisles after the bride with his stupid flash, and extra cameras banging at his side, her posing vapidly, him flashing away, scurrying back with all his contraptions flapping. Would that, could that be me? Please. I hate those shots. What was the purpose of it all anyway? We all know what comes afterwards. The malaise. The control issues. The "communication problems." Her wanting her space. Him wanting more time. The "Other." The "Confrontation in the Restaurant." Oh God. Quiet! I told myself. Get back to the point! The church will be dark. I will need a flash. Lighting by Jonathan won't be enough. I'll have to learn. "Rent Hasselblad and flash" went down on the list. How many months did I have to learn the gear? Add another assistant for the rapid-fire film winding and loading.

That problem somewhat dealt with, I went on to the one which I dreaded even thinking about. Woke up in the night worrying about. Even, in some dreams, devising strange, Star Warsian light wands to solve. The problem of the Family Portraits. In the mansion where the reception would be held, the Grand Hall opened up to a Scarlett O'Hara staircase. There it was that the bride and her mother visualized the family groups gathering and being creatively and inventively posed by me to generate the kind of portraits for which I had, in her eyes, become so esteemed. It would be her dark-haired mother, a classic Revlon beauty, her father, a portly physician, and her sister, a soft blonde beauty as sweet as the bride was hard and bright. These, and who else? The groom, handsome in his morning suit, his frostily elegant English mother in her hat, and her Cary Grant-looking father and their assorted aunties. Who else? Who else. The oaken Victorian stairs, the light, and the cast of characters presented the potential for a gorgeous portrait which, in light of the circumstances—a tidal wave of revelers breaking over the bride—I was one hundred percent sure I could not make. But somehow would.

Then, lest I forget, there was the video, the candids, the toasts, the cake, the dance. Impossible. Was it? There is a particularly sanguine aspect to an almost impossible challenge. It takes your mind off the dailiness of life. Gives you something to do. A place to focus your fear. You go into action because you have no choice. Nothing for it but to do it. After all, you've already spent the advance check!

So I launched into preparation. Becoming a wedding photographer overnight was going to entail months of grueling rehearsal, equipment rental, tryout and experimentation, assistant interviews, lighting tests, practice runs, and prayer. As I worked through the list, visualizing the whole thing, I started to smile. This was going to be fun!

By the day of the wedding, my AMEX card was more tired than I was. Our bank account wavering. I still did not trust the on-camera flash. But all was prepped: three assistants, plus my husband, with his English accent and best dark suit, as People Manager, and a van full of equipment and I. The day would begin with a ride from our home in the dusty back hills of Marin County to the gleaming avenues of Pacific Heights, a beginning that did indeed call to mind *Four Weddings and a Funeral.*

At 10:00 in the morning, we loaded the (borrowed) van. In went a case full of rental Hasselblad cameras, lenses and strobes, my own precious 4x5 view camera, and—who knows, just in case—my Nikons, and even (what the hell) the little point and shoot my father left me. (Daddy, I thought, who never missed a picture, may his Force be with me!) All the rest of the rental gear got checked and loaded: lights, stands, tripods, sandbags, poles, cables, stuff in milk crates, stuff in satchels, and rolls of seamless background paper sticking out the back. Groaning, listing, the van lurched down the drive.

The road over the mountain from our place to the City is the kind people from the East write home about, with Dramamine turns and stomach-in-your-throat subsidences and cliffs dropping off hundreds of feet to the sea. The van screeched and clunked around each turn. I worried, from the sound, about bolts coming loose, and whether the wheels would hold on. But we braved ahead, nervously laughing. Unlike the man in the dark suit with the carnation who was heaving his guts out beside a pink limousine that had pulled over to the edge of the cliff. Poor thing. Maybe a failed wedding photographer? We all laughed.

The poor thing, we learned later, was actually to have been the best man in a wedding that was taking place back in the town where we lived. Halfway over the mountain from the City, nauseous to the eyeballs, he had told the limo driver to halt, let him out, and come back for him after the wedding. And there he stayed, green and heaving, while his friends exchanged vows. Speaking of omens, I wonder how that marriage turned out.

To get a sense of the rest of the day, you must picture a raft trip. There is the beautiful start, where the sun rises slowly, and everything is perfect, and everybody points to the swallows on the white cliffs, and glories in the reflections in the mirror-calm water and expands their hearts in the beauty of nature. Ah, you say. This is good. Then you hear the distant hiss. Just a hiss, which gradually becomes a roar. And then, you see it, the edge, and you can't believe it. And you pray for deliverance, and as you plunge over the edge into the churning, deafening, impossible rapids, your mind goes blank.

We crossed the Golden Gate Bridge with me in a hypnotic state, preliving each sequence of the coming day, and Robert chattering on, telling English jokes, humming English hymns, creating, as is his way, a buffer of words between himself and the peril of the moment.

"You know what terrifies me about these things," he said. "What if something goes wrong. I mean, like, wrong. Did I tell you what happened at Ian's wedding?"

"Who's Ian?"

"Ian. Aunt Betty's son, Ian, you know. Ian? And they were doing it up proper. At the castle. Three hundred people, all beautifully dressed. Champagne poured all day. Then, the bloody photographer—well, maybe it wasn't his fault, maybe it was the lab's ..."

"Oh please, Robert," I said. "Not now."

The buffer I need, in times of stress, is silence. I need to concentrate. To picture each scene as it will likely unfold, framing each photograph in advance, previsualizing, as Ansel Adams used to call it—albeit thinking on another, more sublime scale.

Previsualization works the mental landscape the way a sheepdog works a flock: chasing down details, forming a shape, keeping it all moving within the required frame. The difference is that the sheepdog, charging through real mud, nipping at real shanks, can spy and corral the errant straggler which the imagination, drifting about in the ideal, often overlooks.

Such as Lily. I had chosen her to man (woman?) the video camera because she came recommended as being well-dressed, quiet and efficient. Plus, she had an MFA in film. What could go wrong? "What should I wear?" she had asked, after I'd described the scope and grandeur of the event. "Wear black." I'd said. I told her that my crew and I wear crisp formal black, as befitting the setting, and fade in with the scene. "Look sleek," I said. And here she was, in jeans. Oh, well. At least they were black. And given the rules of the church, as laid down at the rehearsal, by Mrs. Thornton, the church's designated wedding manager, the videographer's job was minimal. She was to position the camera on the balcony to the right of the altar, focus it on the spot where the vows would be exchanged, then, "turn it on, leave, and let it record the event on its own." That bothered me.

"There is a problem with this plan," I said, approaching Mrs. Thornton quietly. Her eyebrows lifted. I smiled—somewhat, the way a dog's tail does in the presence of a threat, "The bride and groom will be in this one spot only for the exchange of vows. All the rest of the time, the marching in, the blessings, the marriage homilies, whatever, will take place out of the frame."

Mrs. Thornton squinted. "I've told you," she enunciated clearly and loudly, as if to a non-English speaking waiter, "she can be there—"she gestured with a long forefinger to the balcony—"to focus, or do whatever she does and then," her eyes drilled into mine, "she must retire from view. That's it."

"But—" The eyebrows went up again.

"If the videographer is seen," she explained with the tone of deep fatigue, "then everyone will be looking at her instead of the bride."

Really?

"And frankly," she continued, in the conspiratorial tones of a Robin Williams in drag, "videos are a waste anyway, don't you think?" I blinked. "You know," she continued, smiling like a mean teacher about to dole out punishment, "someone always does something stupid, and then, forever, that's what they remember of the wedding. That one stupid thing. It's always right there." She tapped her forefinger to her brow, eyes narrowed. "Memory."

I will remember the bride's hotel. Her suite was everything a photographer would have wished for. Spacious rooms, view of the Bay Bridge in one window, mountains in the other, art deco buildings rising in the foreground. Light poured in, gilding the champagne buckets, the Chinese armoires, the marble table tops, the gold picture frames, and the bouquets of roses, both red and white. Women bustled everywhere in various stages of undress. Their faces magazine- cover perfect, thanks to Richard, Hair and Make-up, who presided at a circular table laden with bottles and powders and brushes and palates of colors of every hue for eyes, cheeks, lips, nails, and perhaps other things as well, who knows.

"Boobs? No Boobs?" the bride called out, popping foam falsies in and then out of the bodice of her dress. Richard looked up over his round glasses, pausing with his brush at someone's eyelids, "Boobs for the ceremony. But please, honey—not for the dance!"

Boobs or no, dressed and coifed, the bride was like a painting by Sargent. The gown poured down her in a column of glacial satin that flowed around her feet trailed by a lavish, block-long veil.

As I watched and clicked and worked away, easy and confident with the rental Hassy, firing through roll after roll, with Tom, the first assistant, winding and changing backs with lightning speed, roll after roll, black and white, color, I was breathless with happiness at the gorgeousness framed before me.

That was the smooth glide part of the river ride. Then, as it would, came the sound of the hiss. The gathering speed. The sudden breathlessness. The roar of rapids up ahead. The church!

I remember assembling the groomsmen in a stained-glass windowed staircase. I remember setting up the 4x5 on the rear balcony for the dramatic shot of the altar. I remember sending Jon for water, and then, no, come back, as the Mrs. Thornton was gesturing that The Bride had arrived.

I remember thinking, Oh my God, this is it.

And I remember, just as the bride was about to come in the door, the camera failure. The film back jammed. I saw my husband's face pale in the doorway, and his eyes widened as he saw me trying to unjam the thing. I was thinking, My God. Rapids. White. Death. Boiling foam. Verticality. Action. So, this was what it's like to die, and there was my brain going numb while my faithful body was flailing, grabbing, no, swimming up for air. Stop! No.

I checked the film back. No advance. Try another. Still no.

Am I ruined? Ha! That's why they made backups! I was covered.

I grinned at my husband, lest he faint, and whispered, to my first assistant, whose job was to be at my back at all times, "Get me the other Hassy, Tom!" And before I'd even finished the sentence, the backup camera was in my hand and off I went. Ready for the Entry of the Bride. The biggest baddest rapids of all. It was Boat Eater, Fang, all wrapped in one. I was at the front of the church, in my sleek black suit, with my Hassy and on camera flash (Dear God, let it work!) being inconspicuous but ready to dart out and click the one immortal shot. Was the congregation, now all looking my way, thinking, Who is that woman, and where is the real photographer? Could they see my stomach falling through the floor of my body? But then the doors swung open. In a blaze of glory came The Bride, a vision of satin and smiles. Flash. Smile. Flash. Flash. And the Bride and her father glided past me up the aisle and I disappeared, gloriously happy, into the stairwell on the way to photograph the rest from the balcony, where I got my first bad surprise. Lily.

Lily, on the opposite balcony, was bent over the video camera. In plain view. Oh, God. I tasered her with attention. She did not look up. I screamed at her with my eyes. Nothing. I would have to get her out of there somehow. Turning for the door I collided with the dreaded Mrs. Thornton. "Your videographer is still up there!" she hissed. "I know." I said stupidly.

"She disobeyed!" With an exhalation of fury, she swooshed away. Poor Lily. While disobeying me, was obeying the natural laws of a videographer: follow the event; get it on tape. I knew that, appreciated that, but still... "Lily!" I whispered to her as Mrs. Thornton herded her into the vestibule. "How could you!" Her face a crushed camellia.

"But I didn't understand..."

"What part did you not understand, " I said, as kindly as I could, "when I told you three times and then posed for you on the altar so you could frame the shot?"

"But, but..." I interrupted her and asked the furious Mrs. Thornton to let Lily please just go and correct the camera for the exchange of vows. She would have none of it. "But the bride...!" Lily cried.

"Too bad," said Mrs. Thornton, stomping away. Awful as she was, her job was a worthy one, I understood: to preserve the sanctity of the church, even during a glamorous media event. And so, Inside, in a moment of undisturbed solemnity, the bride and groom exchanged vows, and the video camera recorded the floor.

With that, my whole life started swirling down the stomach-churning whirlpool of this terrible mistake. With their vows not properly recorded, will the marriage be jinxed? Will the couple hate me? Will they pay me! Oh God. As the waters of fear of failure threatened to overcome me. Then, the organ sounded the triumphal march. Down they came. Bride and Groom. Bagpiper. Irish Guards, Hats, Everyone. I grabbed my Nikon, Hassy, one-step, everything, and flowed out of the church ahead of them all, clicking, flashing, buoyed on in the cloud of their joy.

The bagpiper led the Bride and Groom and the rest of the billowing procession down Fillmore Street, to the corner of Broadway. There they crossed into the brilliant sunlight, a choice shot, with the party blazingly back-lit and a full panorama of the Bay out beyond. Down Broadway, with wind and sun in their hair and gowns, the procession could have walked out of a Fellini film. Then the mansion. Up the stairs, past the concrete lions. The grand entrance. The classic portrait shot: the airborne veil, the waltzing hem, the bouquet, the bride and groom-like figures on a cake, waving, shining in the sun. Ah. Yes. Got it all.

The rest is the kind of happy blur you feel when surging down that boiling river, after the rapids. Back in the mansion, the great hall was filled with a roar of voices. Cocktail bars glittered. Champagne corks popped. Glasses broke. Under the Victorian palms, the families jostled themselves into place for their portraits. The Bride and Groom, momentarily serene, posed for posterity on the grand staircase. The guests grouped and grinned. The band—big, trumpety "Chicago" sound—struck up, and the party soared.

Upstairs, Robert and James, the technical assistant, had set up the portrait room just as we rehearsed. Nice dove-grey seamless backdrop. Enough light at sixtieth at five-six. Perfect. Hats off to preparation: Let the revelers come. And they did. In pairs, in groups, alone, in various stages of sobriety, in cinematic attire. Each cluster faced the camera as expected, with their picture-taking smiles pasted on. Then, as the camera seduced them, they moved into pose after pose of amazing variety, surprising each other, themselves—and me. The groomsmen burst into song and heaved the groom into the air. Old women showed their knees. Young women rubbed up against young men and made them roll their eyes. Groups broke into dance. Single men flirted with the lens. Pairs of women dared the lens to look back. Even the shyest person opened like a rose.

I was in heaven. And as I worked, I knew that it had not been the monetary desperation that made me take this job, nor had it been only the challenge: it was my vision of these portraits. These faces, these gowns, images of everyone at this high point, in this great light, giving the camera, and me, their best. So, you might say: But it's only wedding photography. So? As a respected fine art photographer replied, when asked by a student how he "reconciles" his commercial work with his fine art work, "I call it Making a Living," he said, adding, "I highly recommend it!"

12

Gifts from Duxbury Reef

Duxbury Reef, the black-backed leviathan, stretches its tight arm out into open sea as if to be reaching for the setting ball of sun. "Longest shale reef in North America," says the guidebook. The implied power for both beauty and destruction suits this piece of coast that rides on a plate of its own, heading imperceptibly, year by year, up to Washington State. I know this because I once had occasion to phone a geologist in Seattle, and he asked me where I was calling from. "Coastal Marin County," I said. "I know," he said. "From your 415 number. But you'll be up here soon enough," he laughed. "Haw haw!" I liked the fact that where I lived was not only a continent away from everything I knew before but on a separate plate of its own, the Pacific Plate, which was moving north, scraping against the North American Plate and causing disruption from time to time. "Don't worry," he said, "it'll take a while." Nothing like a vantage point of eons to make you feel secure.

High above the reef, I am sitting on the edge of the cliff, down which, after rains, whole chunks of earth collapse, along with Monterey cypresses, topsoil, outbuildings, and the occasional house. I always feel a perverse sense of serenity here. I imagine into a perspective outside of time, as below me, clawing the reef, the waves curl up, turn gold, and throw themselves onto the shimmering kelp where they tangle with the pebbles and then, hissing, recede. Robert and I sat here early on, gazing into the roiling sea with its foam turned golden in the sun's late rays. As I climbed down the rocks to get closer to the surf, he said he saw angels surrounding me. I asked him how many—just to be sure of his clarity of mind. "About sixteen," he said, "and they were bringing you gifts." Who could argue with that?

That was soon after we met. Today, I was feeling low, filled with anxiety about the future, full of doubts in our ability to keep afloat. I would have been happy to see an angel or two, with gifts or without. Instead, as I sat on the cliff, the vision that came to me, stomping out of the waves, was of a young William Tecumseh Sherman, ambitious, adventurous and ten years ahead of the march that would emblazon his name in history. He had just resigned his commission as captain in the Army's Commissary Department and was heading, by ship, into San Francisco to launch for himself a career in banking.

As the story goes at around four in the morning, the ship hit a reef and Sherman found himself wading ashore, waist deep in foam, salt in his good leather boots, sea wrack dragging at his belt. Behind him, in the surf, the proud, three-masted ship, S. S. *Lewis*, was rocking, groaning, breaking apart. Passengers in lifeboats clutching their possessions had already made their way to shore. After doing what he could to help, Sherman scrambled up to a knoll, possibly even near the place where I was now sitting and looked around. It was dark. But he could smell smoke and followed his nose over the rough mesa and came upon a campfire. Three or four grizzled men, wheezing and guffawing, were passing around a bottle. Whiskey. Would he like some whiskey? Definitely. But first, where could he get a boat to San Francisco?

They pointed to the north, where, at the town dock at the mouth of the lagoon, a ship loaded with redwood logs would sail at daybreak. The young Sherman took a warming swig of the bottle, bid the "gentlemen" good night, and made his way down another hill to the dock and the ship where he was taken aboard, along with those shipwreck survivors not wanting to stay on in town. He sat on the damp deck, leaned against a barrel, and pulled off his soaking boots and coat and rested from his ordeal. He woke to shouts and lurching of the hull, and they set sail.

The wind in San Francisco Bay was icy, slicing, and came at an angle that seemed designed to flay the skin right off your face. The great waves lifted and crashed the heavy-loaded ship, and the captain's stomach lurched with each groaning subsidence. Though short in miles, the trip was long in misery, and by nightfall, as adventurer's luck would have it, the ship ran aground. Sherman, still damp from the first wreck of the day, was thrust into a second. He took it in stride. "I found myself in the water," he wrote in his memoirs, "mixed up with pieces of plank and ropes; struck out, swam round to the stern, got on the keel, and clambered up on the side . . . I was not in the least alarmed but thought two shipwrecks in one day not a good beginning for a new, peaceful career."

As I entertained the vision of this stalwart, young curmudgeon who was destined for infamy, I thought he might be seen as an angel in disguise. But what could his travails say to me, other than I'm glad I'm not at sea? And yet, as I watched him, in my inner eye, he was smiling. Cast ashore once, shipwrecked again, he trudged ashore for the second time cheerfully and seemingly bearing hardship no grudge. In fact, he seemed to enjoy it. He "footed it" to the Presidio, he wrote, "a good specimen of a shipwrecked mariner," and secured help for the wrecked ship S.S. Lewis, and then, boots sloshing, went his way to where he was supposed to be staying, wondering, as he wrote in his journals that night, given the possible omen of two shipwrecks in one day, whether "it was best to undertake this new and untried scheme of banking, or to return to New Orleans and hold on to what I then had, a good army commission." Whatever would become of his banking career, he was exhilarated by the challenge of shipwrecks and took hardship in stride, as though everyone should experience a shipwreck at least once. I think of his buoyant courage in contrast to my own fears—fear of failure, fear of loss, fear of hardship—and realize that maybe young Captain Sherman has brought me a gift: to recognize circumstances for what they are, as gifts in themselves, the gifts of experience, gifts of challenge, though they don't always arrive in predictable packages, are there for us to unwrap, with varying results.

Thinking about Sherman, with the present storm raging all around me both meteorologically and psychologically, I find that the waves of distress are not overcoming me. Today I will go through the rain, back to the house, take off my boots and slicker, and settle in where it's warm and friendly, with a fire in the woodstove, and where Robert will have breakfast going. On the way back, pounded with rain, I feel an inner smile: I may not have seen the angels he saw, back then, in the surf, but I feel them around me here now. Every day. I feel their gifts.

Reprieve

In one of the Old Testament stories, the white-bearded God demands from the prophet Abraham that he sacrifice his only son. As no command from God can be refused, Abraham, baffled and grief-stricken, bowed to God's command and prepared to do as he was told. He took his son to the appointed place on the mountain, readied the firewood, tied his son to a great rock, and was about to stab him with a knife when the Lord bellowed out, "Stop!" As I imagine the scene, Abraham's fist went limp, the knife dropped, and he stared up at God, who said something to the effect of, "Just kidding."

I think of that because the real estate man has just called. "Sorry. So sorry," he said. "She was a flake after all." He explained that the buyer had just decided, after all these weeks—walking through, measuring, bringing in her experts, making offers, withdrawing offers, renewing offers, then getting friends to help her with the down payment—it was all just a bit too much for her. As he spoke, a shaft of joy started spreading through me like light from an opening door. "Are you kidding?!" I looked at Robert. We could not stop laughing.

Easter Sunday

This morning's Easter service was set out under the trees. The small congregation was arranged in rows on folding chairs outside the little wooden church, built well over a hundred years ago by the same settlers who rest in the graves behind us.

With the cemetery in the background, the altar was laid upon a hot-tub-sized eucalyptus stump, covered with white linen and calla lilies. The air was lemony, pungent with the tangy essence of eucalyptus buds crushed under foot. Crows cawed in the treetops. The choir's voices blew away on the wind with occasional sheets of music. Random dogs of various sizes and colors wandered pleasantly through the rows. My proper English husband was crisp in his best black suit and yellow silk tie. I wore lavender silk pants and a cream-colored cashmere cape. No hats. Babies all around wore pastel dresses. The priest, a stranger to convention, introduced his Easter sermon with a Lawrence Welkian display from a bottle of "Miracle Bubbles." This, he confessed, was what everyone did as teen-agers in the sixties, in the Haight, to symbolize their hopes and dreams. "Perfect for today," he said, "because Easter is the feast of hope, and the resurrection is a dream come true." He called on the older members among us to remember the dreams of their youth. And then, "For those in middle life," he said, making sweeping gestures toward the majority, "who may be in crisis," significant pause with meaningfully widened eyes, waiting for the acknowledging nods and shrugs among those for whom the description applied, "hold on to your dreams. Hold on."

He said more. Something about the littlest members among us being the dreams for the future, but I wasn't listening. I was thinking about all the other "middles" around us, all dressed up in the bright noon light, some of whose struggles I knew. A young man with brain cancer. A mother in her thirties with leukemia. A couple whose kid has drug problems. Families with sons far off in warring countries. Our friend from the garden party, whose house is in foreclosure. People of all sorts, just sitting together as people for a quiet moment in the sunshine, being recognized for what it means to be dealing with life in the nineties.

The priest waved his bubbles, and I thought of the settlers resting in the graveyard behind us who all came, as we did, each from afar, following dreams. Was it easier for them? A stroll through the family plots, past the many little babies' headstones, would suggest not. From a certain distance, all pain, like all grief, is somehow the same. Up close, as with the names and dates on the stones, it is always unique. Impossible to compare or stratify. Sometimes, when I'm enjoying a certain clarity, I think of pain as like a sculptor's tool that shapes who we become.

Thinking of suffering, I focus in on my husband, sitting closely beside me in the sun. He'd given up family and community—a whole country really—to build a life and a company here in California with me. And how different this morning would be back in his home in England, where the church would be stone, built in the eleventh century, and people would be dressed in the manner they all understood and would behave as they have behaved in church for generations. There would be security in sameness—in song. There, people know their place. They know how to define each other. They instinctively recognize which square pegs do not fit the traditional round holes. Robert never talks about going back.

Thinking of England made me think about lunch, and I took his hand as the priest was giving the last blessing.

Later that day, after lunch in the café and a long walk on the beach, we climbed up on the reef, chilled now, in the fading light. I followed him along the slimy slippery rocks, as step by conscious step we made our way along the base of the cliff, just out of the reach of the waves. We stopped for a moment, looking ahead, way up at the top of the cliff, at a giant cypress clinging to the edge, holding on, with half of its great roots dangling over the edge like anemones' tentacles, as if reaching for some sustenance, some grounding in the fog, while the other half goes deep, holds on, draws life from what it has left of the earth. Looking at the tree, I think: *That's me. That's all of us. Holding on, letting go. Half in earth, half in heaven, doomed in time but loving each other, and at home on earth wherever we are.*

My beloved looked down at me and smiled.

"Let's go home."

NOTES

[page 17]
"The Russian philosopher Gurdieff is said to have advised: To learn to love, begin with plants. Spare animals and other humans the insult of our expectations. Love needs acceptance." No direct quote but references to love and plants. —G. I. Gurdjieff, *Views from the Real World* (1973), New York: E. P. Dutton & Co., p. 210.

[page 33]
"I went to the woods because I wished to live deliberately, to front only the essential facts of life, and see if I could not learn what it had to teach, and not, when I came to die, discover that I had not lived." —*Walden*, Henry D. Thoreau
https://www.gutenberg.org/files/205/205-h/205-h.htm#chap03

[page 39]
"…the history of the living world can be summarized as the elaboration of ever more perfect eyes within a cosmos in which there is always something more to be seen." "The work of human works is to establish, in and by means of each one of us, an absolutely original center in which the universe reflects itself in a unique and inimitable way."
— Pierre Teilhard de Chardin, "Forword," *The Phenomenon of Man* (1959), Wm Collins & Sons.

[page 40]
"Yes, the springtimes needed you… "The First Elegy," translation copyright © 1982 by Stephen Mitchell; from SELECTED POETRY OF RAINER MARIA RILKE by Rainer Maria Rilke, edited and translated by Stephen Mitchell. Used by permission of Random House, an imprint and division of Penguin Random House LLC. All rights reserved.

[page 68]
A NASA team of scientists had—believe it or not—recently performed experiments where groups of spiders were fed, respectively, Benzedrine, caffeine, and marijuana.
"Nasa Experiment with Spiders and Mind-Altering Drugs" https://www.miragenews.com/nasas-experiment-with-spiders-mind-altering-996703/

[page 86]
"The stars throw well. One can help them."
—Loren Eiseley, *The Star Thrower* (1978), The Estate of Loren C. Eiseley, Times Books, p. 172.

[page 155]
This information from the *Memoirs of General Sherman, The Project Gutenberg eBook of the Memoirs of General W. T. Sherman, Complete,* by William T. Sherman. Chap IV 1850-18-55.

ABOUT THE AUTHOR

Bonnie Durrance, born and brought up in Washington D. C., has made it her mission to live and work in places that called to her soul: on the western shore of the Chesapeake Bay, as a teacher; on the Coast of Maine, as a photographer; back to the cities, Washington, D. C. and New York, as a producer of multi-media installations for museums and corporate clients; then on to the coast of West Marin, California, where she returned to her love of writing and fine art photography. Now, she works and makes her home beside the Napa River in the Napa Valley with her husband, Robert, six chickens, numerous coyotes, and other wild things.

SHANTI ARTS

NATURE · ART · SPIRIT

Please visit us online
to browse our entire book catalog,
including poetry collections and fiction,
books on travel, nature, healing, art,
photography, and more.

Also take a look at our highly regarded art
and literary journal, *Still Point Arts Quarterly*,
which may be downloaded for free.

www.shantiarts.com

www.ingramcontent.com/pod-product-compliance
Lightning Source LLC
Chambersburg PA
CBHW042146160426
43202CB00023B/2991